THE
CREATOR'S
CODE

The Six Essential Skills of
Extraordinary Entrepreneurs

Amy Wilkinson

SIMON & SCHUSTER

New York   London   Toronto   Sydney   New Delhi

Simon & Schuster
1230 Avenue of the Americas
New York, NY 10020

First Simon & Schuster hardcover edition February 2015

SIMON & SCHUSTER and colophon are registered trademarks of
Simon & Schuster, Inc.

For information about special discounts for bulk purchases, please
contact Simon & Schuster Special Sales at 1-866-506-1949 or
business@simonandschuster.com.

The Simon & Schuster Speakers Bureau can bring authors to your live
event. For more information or to book an event, contact the
Simon & Schuster Speakers Bureau at 1-866-248-3049 or visit
our website at www.simonspeakers.com.

Interior design by Claudia Martinez
Jacket design by Julius Reyes

Manufactured in the United States of America

10 9 8 7 6 5 4 3 2 1

ISBN 978-1-4767-9109-8
ISBN 978-1-4516-6609-0 (ebook)

Dedicated to things that haven't happened yet
and the dreamers who will make them come true

CONTENTS

THE CREATOR'S CODE

Introduction

CRACKING THE CODE

Kevin Plank was kicked out of prep school, bounced into a military academy, and saw his dreams of playing college football seemingly vanish when not a single Division I school recruited him. But in 1991, he muscled his way on to the University of Maryland's football team as a walk-on fullback.

Plank worked harder on the field than others. He had to. He hustled and put his head down to jolt opponents. Eric Ogbogu, a six-foot-four, 245-pound Maryland defensive lineman who went on to play for the New York Jets, the Cincinnati Bengals, and the Dallas Cowboys, often tells people he suffered only one concussion during his college career, and it came compliments of the five-foot-eleven, 228-pound Plank.

Plank perspired a lot. One day, he weighed the sweat-soaked cotton T-shirt he wore under his uniform and discovered that it added three pounds to his weight. Smaller and less athletic than his Division I teammates, he couldn't afford to be slowed down by his gear. Could a less absorbent undershirt provide an edge?

Plank found a fabric store near the Maryland campus in College Park and explained what he wanted. Synthetic fabrics, he learned, wick away sweat more effectively than cotton. Plank bought a bolt of a stretchy microfiber material, found a local tailor, and had a T-shirt made. It took seven prototypes and $450, but he got what he wanted: a snug T-shirt that weighed three ounces dry and only seven ounces wet.

Plank gave his teammates samples of the shirt. After their next game, they raved about it.

"The little-known secret behind Under Armour geared for tough football players is that it's the same material as women's lingerie," Plank said with a smile.

After graduation, Plank drove his Ford Bronco to New York City's Garment District to track down a fabric supplier. He found a small mill in Ohio willing to manufacture his shirts. He called every equipment manager in the Atlantic Coast Conference (Maryland's home athletic league at that time) and went locker room to locker room, handing out samples of his moisture-wicking shirts. Working from his grandmother's basement in Washington, D.C., Plank and a friend, Kip Fulks, hustled twenty hours a day, chasing orders and boxing shipments.

"Yes, it was difficult," Plank told me, "but I never believed it wasn't possible." Despite burning through $17,000, every cent of his savings, and amassing $40,000 in credit-card debt, he didn't stop. When Nike representatives dismissed his products at trade shows, he began sending Nike cofounder Phil Knight an annual Christmas card with the message, "You haven't heard about us yet, but you will."

Soon orders started coming in: Plank made his first sizable sale to Georgia Tech, and North Carolina State followed. When the Atlanta Falcons called to ask whether Plank could fill orders for long-sleeve shirts, he responded, "Of course!" then scrambled to figure out how. Next, baseball, lacrosse, and rugby players wanted Under Armour gear. Before long, a company started by a football player for football players even began serving the women's market. Today, Under Armour is a $2.9 billion global brand.

Plank isn't an expert in fabrics or manufacturing, or even retail. He never played a down in the National Football League. He doesn't hold a degree from an Ivy League school. He is a creator who has cracked the creator's code.

"What defines our brand is that there is this blue-collar, this walk-on mentality, that there is nothing that can stop me, there is nothing that can prevent me from moving forward to being success-ful," Plank said as we walked across Under Armour's campus in a gritty Baltimore neighborhood.

THE ROAD TO RAMEN PROFITABILITY

In 2007, on the other side of the United States, Joe Gebbia received a letter from the landlord of his San Francisco apartment: "Dear Joe: Your rent has gone up 25 percent." Gebbia and roommate Brian Chesky wondered how they were going to afford it.

Recent graduates of the Rhode Island School of Design, they planned to attend the Industrial Designers Society of America con-ference that week. While looking at the conference organizers' Web site, they happened to see a notice: "Sorry, the hotels are sold out. There are no more rooms in San Francisco." Surveying their living room, the two designers realized they had space where they could put people up, but no extra beds. "I have an airbed in the closet," Gebbia told Chesky.

Inspiration had struck. They inflated the bed, along with two others borrowed from friends, and started to think about the experience they would want paying guests to have. What if they picked them up from the airport? Why not put mints on the pillows? What if they cooked breakfast for their guests? Then they had the name. It wasn't a bed-and-breakfast; it was an airbed-and-breakfast. Airbnb was born.

"It was a delight hosting Kat, Emil, and Michael" that inaugural weekend, Gebbia said, remembering the first three people to check into their airbed hostelry. The positive experience, extra cash, and connection with their guests got Gebbia and Chesky wondering what would happen if they encouraged others to rent out their spaces.

The duo brought on computer programmer Nathan Blecharczyk to help build Airbnb. Their target market: conference-goers.

In the beginning, they made just $200 a week. But the struggle made them more frugal and creative. During the 2008 presidential campaign, the designers crafted limited-edition boxes of breakfast cereals they named "Obama O's—Hope in Every Bowl" and "Cap'n McCain's—A Maverick in Every Bite." They initially gave them to bloggers for publicity, then marketed them for $40 a box. They sold out, generating $25,000, which kept Airbnb afloat. "It was so not in the playbook of how to start a company," Gebbia said with a chuckle.

Airbnb reached "Ramen profitability" in 2010. Gebbia explained: "It's the moment when you're making enough in revenue to pay your rent and eat Top Ramen. If you can get to that moment, you have an unlimited runway."

On any given night, more than 200,000 travelers in 34,000 cities across 192 countries stay in Airbnb rooms. By comparison, Hilton has 600,000 rooms worldwide. In April 2014, not long after Gebbia met me wearing a hoodie, thick-framed glasses, and red sneakers at Airbnb's headquarters in San Francisco, the company secured $450 million in additional capital. The analysis that clinched the investment put the company's worth at $10 billion, making it one of the world's most valuable startups.

DREAMERS WHO DO

Brian Chesky, Joe Gebbia, and Nathan Blecharczyk figured out a way to rent out space, use technology, and create a company that would not only solve their particular problem—the high cost of housing—but also empower others to participate in the solution. And their company grew, just like Under Armour.

Starting a sharing-economy company wasn't trendy or cool. No venture capitalist clamored to fund "the weird idea" to rent couches and extra bedrooms to strangers. The Airbnb founders' idea was a long shot. Or was it?

Chesky, Gebbia, and Blecharczyk were like a lot of people. They came across a business concept they believed in. It wasn't awe inspiring, but it had strong appeal. The idea was promising but not foolproof. Still, they dreamed it could work. "There was something that lived inside of us, a spirit we couldn't shake," Gebbia explained. "There was this logic all around us telling us to stop, but there was something inside us we couldn't ignore."

Each of us has that ability to identify opportunities, invent products, and build businesses—even $100 million businesses. We can influence how the future unfolds. We can create.

A new generation of dreamers is doing just that—turning ordinary ideas into extraordinary enterprises. These men and women—defined by their mastery of the six essential skills described in this book—have cracked the creator's code. They prove that a little daring and discipline can go a long way, and that entrepreneurship is accessible to everyone.

Creators don't strive to be first the way a top student does. Rather, they seek to be *only*—the only one to see a need, spot a new use for an existing technology, or devise an original solution. Curiosity supersedes credentials.

In the past, we used assembly-line approaches to business and education. The old way was to solve an equation, then replicate the solution. That kind of linear thinking supports a standardized process. But creators recognize that no perfect equation for success exists in the tumult of today's economy. They invent new ways forward.

Creators don't need an MBA, millions of dollars, perfect timing, or permission. They don't need years of experience. Peter Thiel, Max Levchin, and Elon Musk, creators who founded online payment giant PayPal, were not bankers. Steve Chen, Chad Hurley, and Jawed Karim, founders of YouTube, were not video experts. Hamdi Ulukaya, who built Chobani, the leading Greek yogurt brand in the United States, had never operated a manufacturing plant. Sara Blakely, creator of Spanx, a billion-dollar business that sells body-shaping undergarments, started as a door-to-door fax machine saleswoman.

Creators discover what ignites them, then fuel their efforts with a sense of mission that transcends the bottom line. "Certainly our passion is bigger than burritos and tacos. I want to change the way people eat fast food," said Steve Ells, founder of fast-casual restaurant Chipotle. "Taking life to Mars is as important as life going from oceans to land," Elon Musk, founder of space exploration company SpaceX, told me. "There are no slam dunks," said Alex Laskey, cofounder of Opower, which sells energy-saving software. "Might as well fail trying to do something important."

In this book, you'll discover how today's entrepreneurial exemplars achieve meaningful results. You'll come to understand why Reid Hoffman, cofounder of career networking site LinkedIn, says you must "throw yourself off a cliff and assemble an airplane on the way down. Good startup entrepreneurs are extremely aware of the impact of time because with each second, you are closer to the ground. The whole thing is about building an airplane that is self-sustaining." You'll learn how Robin Chase, cofounder of car-sharing business Zipcar, started her company as a forty-two-year-old mother of three to provide "wheels when you want them." And you'll discover why Jeremy Stoppelman, cofounder of business review site Yelp, didn't expect that the first thing he tried would work but instead looked for "a counterintuitive blip of data to explore further."

How are these men and women changing the way we live? What tools, traits, practices, and habits help them to succeed? The search for answers to those questions led to this book.

THE NEXT STEVE JOBS

Elizabeth Holmes dropped out of Stanford University at age nineteen to start a company. Fascinated by microfluidics and nanotechnology, she envisioned a way to revolutionize laboratory testing to make diagnostic tests faster, cheaper, less painful, and more accurate. Today, Theranos, the company she founded, is poised to shake up the lab testing industry by increasing the speed and quality of health care while bringing down costs. Tomorrow, it may do much more, helping to accelerate medical treatments and, ultimately, prevent diseases by finding their telltale signs before they can take hold.

"The reality is that when someone you love gets really sick, nothing matters more, and yet we often find cancer only after tumors have formed and spread. It's heartbreaking," Holmes said. "I don't think it should be that way."

Holmes started Theranos in 2003, using her tuition money as capital. She worked from the basement of a college group house to invent a small yet sophisticated fingerstick device that can draw a few drops of blood into a tiny "nanotainer." But the more profound innovation concerns what happens next. "We had to develop assays or test methodologies that would accelerate results," Holmes told me. "The traditional method in the case of a virus or bacteria is to test using a culture. We measure the DNA of a pathogen to get much faster results."

In the fall of 2013, Holmes announced a partnership with Walgreens that will put Theranos in more than 8,200 locations nationwide. Instead of visiting a doctor's office to have blood drawn and waiting days for the result, patients can stop at their local pharmacy and have results delivered electronically to physicians the same day. The cost is less than half the standard Medicare and Medicaid reimbursement rates for traditional lab work. What's more, Theranos presents test results in easy-to-read digital graphs that doctors and patients can quickly access online and through mobile applications.

For all that Theranos may be able to do for American health care in the next few years, it's not enough for Holmes. "The dream is to present actionable information to physicians and patients in time to do something in a way in which prevention becomes possible," she said. "There's not a higher purpose that I could aim for."

THE SIX ESSENTIAL SKILLS

How does a college dropout build a technology with the potential to revolutionize the health-care field? How do two cash-strapped San Francisco designers build a breakout sharing-economy business? What makes a University of Maryland football player turn his sweaty problem into a global sports brand? The unlikely stories of these creators are surprising only because no one has cracked the code that explains how these iconoclasts gain traction to achieve lasting results.

Until now.

The Creator's Code is based on interviews with 200 entrepreneurs who have started companies that generate more than $100 million in annual revenue or social enterprises that serve more than 100,000 people. Some of these creators have started businesses that generate more than $1 billion in revenue every year.

Crisscrossing the country, I spent hours interviewing creators in technology, retail, energy, health care, media, mobile applications, biotechnology, real estate, travel, and hospitality, working to understand their approach. Across my research, I witnessed individuals turning small notions into big companies time and again.

From the creators who invented online storage provider Dropbox (annual revenue $200 million), fast-casual restaurant chain Chipotle ($3.9 billion), discount airline JetBlue ($5.7 billion), to a myriad of other successful businesses, I found that they achieved entrepreneurial success in much the same way.

Without exception, creators describe their work as doing something much more than achieving financial ambitions—they aim to make a mark on the world. "This generation of technologists thinks about bringing people together to do all sorts of interesting things," eBay founder Pierre Omidyar told me. "That's intoxicating and incredibly motivating and creates a stage of human development that is fundamentally new."

Analyzing nearly 10,000 pages of interview transcripts and more than 5,000 pieces of archival and documentary evidence, I worked to understand how creators, sometimes dismissed as unrealistic dreamers, not only come to disrupt competitors but also to reshape entire industries. The research is based on grounded theory method, widely used in qualitative analysis. My extensive interviews were recorded and the resulting transcripts combed for common attributes that were coded and then grouped into concepts. These results allowed me to identify the categories that provide the basis for developing the theory of six essential skills that enable the success of every creator.

To test and support my conclusions, I immersed myself in the literature relevant to entrepreneurial endeavor from the fields of organizational behavior, psychology, sociology, entrepreneurship, economics, strategy, decision theory, and creativity. I reviewed more than 4,000 pages of academic research, examined hundreds of studies and experiments, and consulted leading scholars. (For more on my research methodology, please see the appendix.)

It was a five-year odyssey that led me to six skills that make creators successful.

Creators are not born with an innate ability to conceive and build $100 million enterprises. They work at it. I found that they all share certain fundamental approaches to the act of creation. The skills that make them successful can be learned, practiced, and passed on. Each is the topic of a chapter in this book:

1. FIND THE GAP

By staying alert, creators spot opportunities that others don't see. They keep their eyes open for fresh potential, a vacuum to fill, or an unmet need. Creators tend to use one of three distinct techniques: transplanting ideas across divides, designing a new way forward, or merging disparate concepts. I characterize creators who master these approaches as Sunbirds, Architects, or Integrators.

2. DRIVE FOR DAYLIGHT

Just as race-car drivers keep their eyes fixed on the road ahead, creators focus on the future, knowing that where they go, their eyes go first. Creators move too fast to navigate by the confines of their lane or the position of their peers. Instead, they focus on the horizon, scan the edges, and avoid nostalgia to set the pace in a fast-moving marketplace.

3. FLY THE OODA LOOP

Creators continuously update their assumptions. In rapid succession, they observe, orient, decide, and act. Like legendary fighter pilot John Boyd, who pioneered the idea of the "OODA loop," creators move nimbly from one decision to the next. They master fast-cycle iteration and in short order gain an edge over less agile competitors.

4. FAIL WISELY

Creators understand that experiencing a series of small failures is essential to avoiding catastrophic mistakes. In the course of practicing and mastering this skill, they set what I call failure ratios, place small bets to test ideas, and develop resilience. They hone the skill to turn setbacks into successes.

5. NETWORK MINDS

To solve multifaceted problems, creators bring together the brainpower of diverse individuals through on- and off-line forums. They harness cognitive diversity to build on each other's ideas. To do this, creators design shared spaces, foster flash teams, hold prize competitions, and build work-related games. They collaborate with unlikely allies.

6. GIFT SMALL GOODS

Creators unleash generosity by helping others, often by sharing information, pitching in to complete a task, or opening opportunities to colleagues. Offering kindness may not seem like a skill, but it is an essential way that creators strengthen relationships. In an increasingly transparent and interconnected world, generosity makes creators more productive.

The six essential skills are not discrete, stand-alone practices. Each feeds the next, creating synergy and momentum. The diagram below demonstrates how the skills connect and build on each other.

No special expertise is required to master the six skills. You don't need credentials or degrees. The ability to turn ideas into enduring enterprises is available to anyone willing to learn and work. Although everyone has strengths in certain skills and weaknesses in others, the more we exercise and increase our proficiency in each, the more we will be able to make the most of every opportunity.

When a creator brings together all six skills, something magnetic occurs. Creators attract allies—employees, customers, investors, and collaborators of all kinds. Customers become evangelists.

Employees turn into loyalists. Investors back the company with support that transcends financial returns.

The pages ahead show how a creator can make all kinds of endeavors succeed. Creators engage in meaningful work with the aim of making a difference. To become one of them, all you need is to understand and practice the six essential skills.

Chapter 1

FIND THE GAP

Discovery consists in seeing what everyone else has seen
and thinking what no one else has thought.

—Albert Szent-Györgyi

From an early age, Elon Musk peppered his parents with questions. He prodded and probed. "Guess I'm just wired that way," he told me. Born in Pretoria, South Africa, Musk devoured comic books and science-fiction novels as a youth. He read the encyclopedia cover to cover. He loved computers. At the age of ten, he taught himself how to write computer code; by the time he was twelve, he and his brother, Kimbal, had developed and sold a video game, set in outer space, called Blaster. *The Hitchhiker's Guide to the Galaxy*, a comedic science-fiction novel, taught him to question accepted wisdom; as is memorably written in the book, the key is to know which questions to ask.

Musk's curiosity fueled his desire to move to the United States. "America is a nation of explorers," he said. First, he moved to Canada to stay with relatives. To pay for college, he worked odd jobs: shoveling grain, emptying boilers in a lumber mill, mopping up chemicals while wearing a hazmat suit. He graduated from the University of Pennsylvania, where he asked professors, classmates, friends, and even dates this question: "What are the three things that will have the greatest impact on the future of humanity?"

By 1995, Musk realized that "the Internet was like humanity acquiring a nervous system," he said. "Previously, we'd been like cells connecting by osmosis. We were just a blob. But if you have a nervous system, information can travel instantly from the tip of your finger to your mind, and then down to your feet. The Internet turns humanity into something akin to a superorganism."

Musk enrolled in a PhD program in applied physics at Stanford University, but he dropped out after just two days. He was far more interested in pursuing the gap he perceived between the potential of the Internet and the way it was being used at the time. He sent his résumé to America Online (AOL)—a hot company in the mid-1990s—made follow-up calls, and even drove to the company's office, hanging around the lobby hoping someone would talk with him. No one did.

With $2,000 in savings, he and Kimbal started Zip2, one of the first businesses to put media content online. They rented an office and, to save money, furnished it with futons they used as couches during the day and beds at night. They showered at a local gym. "Do you think you'll ever replace this?" one potential investor scoffed, throwing a copy of the Yellow Pages at the brothers. Musk nodded and left. Within months, Zip2 would put maps and content online for media organizations such as the New York Times Company and the Hearst Corporation. Four years later, in 1999, Compaq's Alta-Vista division bought Zip2 for more than $300 million.

With newfound money in his account, Musk turned to the problem of checks, which he saw as a painfully antiquated means of payment. Transactions could take weeks to complete as people mailed checks and waited for them to clear. Musk launched an online payments company called X.com to fill the gap. Before long, it merged with a startup named Confinity to become PayPal. In 2002, eBay purchased PayPal for $1.5 billion. Musk was just getting started.

He would go on to found SpaceX, Tesla Motors, and SolarCity. What can we learn from such an extraordinary creator? What allows someone like Musk to seize opportunities time and again?

Connections, expertise, talent, and resources have something to do with a breakthrough discovery, to be sure, yet scores of people who possess all these ingredients fail to capture opportunities. And individuals who possess few of them succeed. What if the answer involves unique ways of thinking and perceiving? What if Musk—and others like him—have a sensibility and a curiosity that allow them to identify needs that are going unmet?

This chapter is about what makes creators different, what makes them able to find and fill gaps in a variety of ways. Some of these creators—those I call *Sunbirds*—transport solutions that work in one area and apply them to another, often with a twist. *Architects* recognize openings and furnish what is missing. They spot problems and design new products and services to satisfy unfilled needs. Melding existing concepts to combine disparate approaches, *Integrators* build blended outcomes.

Although our experience may lead us to see the world from just one of these perspectives, we can learn to spot opportunities in a variety of ways. Creators move freely between patterns of discovery.

SUNBIRDS: FROM ONE DOMAIN TO ANOTHER

"I look at a problem and think, 'Let's not look at how this problem has been approached in this field, but let's go to industries that are completely different and take technologies that, if applied to the problem at hand, would solve it,'" inventor Dean Kamen said. Kamen created the Segway PT transportation vehicle, the AutoSyringe drug infusion pump, and the iBOT all-terrain wheelchair, among other technologies. "I find someone who has solved the problem in another field and then just tweak it a little bit," Kamen explained, adding wryly, "Every once in a while it works."

Kamen is a real-life mad scientist. He lives in a large, hexagonal house in Bedford, New Hampshire, that features, among other quirks, a large steam engine once owned by Henry Ford. Kamen pilots his own helicopter to work every day. The helicopter inspired Kamen, Sunbird-style, to invent a heart stent. Baxter Healthcare, frustrated with stents that collapsed inside blood vessels, commissioned Kamen to create a sturdier model. Helicopter blades withstand incredible stress, so Kamen studied their function and construction and applied what he learned to build a better stent.

Kamen spots a solution that works in one area and repurposes it. Designing the Segway PT, he borrowed gyroscopic technology used in the aerospace industry to maintain stability. Kamen utilized two sets of wheels capable of rotating over each other to enable users of his iBOT wheelchair to "walk" up a flight of stairs or "stand" up to six feet tall. His Luke Arm prosthetic device—named after the Star Wars character Luke Skywalker—gives its wearer a nearly full range of motion. It is designed with fourteen sensors that detect temperature and pressure and enable users to open a lock with a key or grip a water bottle.

Perhaps his greatest invention is FIRST (For Inspiration and Recognition of Science and Technology), a nonprofit that borrows from the playbook of sports to make math and science education cool. "I got this epiphany to create a sport of technology and science that had a higher skill set than 'bounce, bounce, and throw,'" Kamen explained. Borrowing on the sports theme of instant winners and losers, he designed a six-week science and technology tournament in which teams of students face off in robotics competitions that require them to build a robot out of a box of standard components. "If you want to see a real varsity team, I'll show you a real sport," Kamen quipped. "The other neat thing is that whether you're three hundred pounds, seven feet tall, or a woman, you can play on the same team." In 2014, more than 400,000 students participated in FIRST competitions.

What makes someone a Sunbird? The first and most obvious criterion is that Sunbirds take something that already exists and transport the model to create something new. They relocate and reshape existing concepts across geographies and industries, and bring old ideas up to date.

By definition, a sunbird is a small bird native to Africa, Asia, and parts of Australia. Like the North American hummingbird, sunbirds subsist primarily on nectar. They fly from bud to bud, transferring pollen between flowers.

There is a simple way to describe how Sunbird creators spot opportunities. They harvest working concepts, proving that repurposing an idea can be a powerful means of discovery. Sunbirds transport solutions from one place to meet the needs of another.

Starbucks CEO Howard Schultz, for example, didn't invent the espresso bar—he borrowed it. But Schultz was alert enough to envision the coffee bar concept in another locale, and insightful enough to bring it to the United States.

On a business trip to Italy, Schultz was intrigued to find people gathering at local cafés, drinking espresso and enjoying the company of neighbors. "These places offered comfort, community, and a sense of extended family," he said. It was an important part of the culture in cities such as Milan. At the time, if Americans had a cup of coffee while out and about, it was probably at a diner. Schultz spotted the "third place" coffeehouse tradition: the café as a public place to gather between work and home. That kind of place was missing in the United States. Schultz saw an opportunity to transplant a winning idea.

But he didn't get it exactly right the first time. With Il Giornale, Schultz's first attempt to open espresso bars in the United States, he replicated the Italian café experience exactly, right down to waiters in bow ties and opera playing in the background. He realized quickly, however, that his Seattle customers didn't enjoy the experience. So he tweaked the concept: jazz and blues replaced the opera; seating was added so customers didn't have to stand at a bar to drink their coffee. Driving the makeover was Schultz's realization that Americans wanted a setting where they could feel comfortable working at their laptops while they sipped coffee.

Sunbirds identify a working concept and find a way to plug it in elsewhere. They examine how and why it worked initially, and what similarities or differences will make it work again. Sunbirds such as Schultz make the calculation repeatedly.

Starbucks VIA instant coffee originated from another Sunbird leap. The process used to preserve the full-bodied taste of coffee beans in powder form was derived from a medical technology invented to preserve blood cells. Biologist Don Valencia presented Schultz with a cup of instant coffee made from freeze-dried concentrate that Valencia had processed in his lab. It turns out that Valencia had developed a technology to freeze-dry blood cells, and he found that the same method could be applied to coffee. Thrilled with the crossover discovery, Schultz hired Valencia to run Starbucks' research and development team. In its first year, Starbucks VIA captured 30 percent of the premium single-serve coffee market in the United States.

The farther Sunbirds transport solutions, the greater the likelihood of breakthrough results. Gaps can be narrow, leading to incremental innovations, or they can be wide, leading to more novel creations.

THE POWER OF ANALOGY

To transport concepts that the rest of us don't see, Sunbirds use the power of analogy.

Analogy operates on two levels: *Surface* analogies describe similarities such as shared product design and product features, and *structural* analogies reflect parallel underlying elements.

Howard Schultz drew a surface analogy when he observed coffee culture in Europe and brought the coffeehouse experience to the United States. When Schultz invested in technology that originally was developed to freeze-dry red blood cells and created VIA instant coffee, he followed a structural analogy.

The odds of success for a Sunbird improve if concepts and applications share structural similarities. Gutenberg is said to have invented the printing press by adapting the mechanics of the wine press. He witnessed the repeated pressing process farmers used to extract juice from grapes and realized that the same mechanism could be utilized to apply ink to paper.

Sunbirds examine underlying elements. George de Mestral got the idea for Velcro when he observed how burrs stuck to his dog's fur with tiny hooks. University of Oregon track coach Bill Bowerman studied his wife's waffle iron and adapted the pattern of little spikes produced by the appliance to create Nike's original waffle-tread running shoe.

It is not always as easy as it might seem to identify and transport ideas. The Inca people of South America fashioned toy vehicles for their children that had wheels, yet they never developed full-scale wheeled carts or wagons. Instead, they used pack animals, and moved heavy items by dragging them on poles. The Incas predicted seasons by observing the planets and stars. Their surgeons were highly skilled. They designed complex roads and buildings with their skilled use of mathematics. Yet they were unable to make the connection between wheels on toy vehicles and their own need for transportation.

"If you take a minute to really think about things, to compare and contrast, you are two to three times as likely to apply known principles to discover and connect with future ideas," said Dedre Gentner, director of the Cognitive Science Program at Northwestern University. Energetic engagement triggers the brain to recast what we see into new and useful ideas. Through experiments with management consultants, accountants, business school students, and undergraduates, Gentner found that making comparisons helps people utilize what they already know. "Push your analogies to the limit. That will lead to breakthroughs," Gentner said. "Instead of saying, 'Damn, that didn't work,' ask, 'What parallel can I draw?'"

"When I finished my doctorate in engineering, I did something very unusual for an engineer. I actually started in a surgery lab," Bob Langer, founder of the Langer Lab at the Massachusetts Institute of Technology, told me. "I was trying to use engineering to solve medical problems." Transporting chemical engineering principles to the human body, Langer helped isolate an angiogenesis inhibitor, capable of choking off the blood supply to cancerous cells, and then invented a new polymer that could be used to encapsulate the treatment, allowing it to be implanted directly in a tumor, where it would be slowly released. His breakthrough created an entirely new kind of drug delivery system that is now a key weapon in fighting cancer and other ills, from diabetes to schizophrenia.

At MIT, Langer runs the largest academic biomedical engineering lab in the world. It has spun out more than twenty-five biotech startups that have each generated more than $100 million in revenue. Langer gets his inspiration from all types of sources, including nature, literature, media, and science, among dozens of others. To create a recent invention, Langer drew an analogy from the computer industry. "The whole idea started by watching a television show on how they make microchips in the computer industry," Langer said, as we sat on lab stools surrounded by centrifuges. "When I saw that, I put two and two together and thought, well, maybe this could be a whole new way of delivering drugs to patients."

The polymer chip is patterned after an Intel microprocessor. "You can open up specific wells in the microchip to deliver drugs," Langer explained. The human microchip works via a tiny device that can be implanted in a patient in the doctor's office. The device is wirelessly programmable by means of a special radio frequency. A signal is sent from a cell phone or other external device that tells the chip what drug to deliver and when, while recording the action. "It can be triggered by remote control the same way you open your garage door," Langer said, using another analogy to describe how it works. This "pharmacy on a chip" was used successfully to administer daily doses of an osteoporosis drug to patients in 2012. Treatment of osteoporosis can require daily injections, whereas the use of an internal microchip could open a new era of easy, pain-free treatment.

Making another Sunbird leap, Langer drew inspiration from a

gecko's foot in creating a surgical bandage capable of holding tissue together inside the body. He designed a glue-coated polymer based on the lizard's wall-gripping ability that can cling snugly to tissue. The result is an adhesive bandage that may replace traditional methods of closing surgical wounds, such as staples. The bandage adheres to uneven surfaces and dissolves harmlessly in the body.

Sunbirds don't allow social or market stigmas about how things get done in a certain field to dictate the way something might be repurposed. But Sunbirds don't only spot opportunity by transplanting current ideas. They also revive outdated concepts to bring them up to date.

People have held garage sales almost as long as there have been garages. That didn't stop Pierre Omidyar, a twenty-eight-year-old software engineer, from beginning to update the concept in 1997. "What I set out to do was to take something that worked really well in the off-line world—namely trade and commerce—and bring it to the online world," said Omidyar, founder of eBay. A Sunbird analogy was at the heart of the original eBay concept.

"One of the things I tend to do is open myself up to a variety of voices—not just the smartest strategists, and the most brilliant people, but just normal, everyday folks as well," Omidyar told me. "I try to expose myself to the kind of culture shock that occurs when you talk to people who speak a different language."

Similarly, Craig Newmark brought traditional classified ads forward in time by creating Craigslist. Jessica Herrin, founder of Stella & Dot, updated Mary Kay's direct-sales model to build a $220 million business that supports 16,000 women selling jewelry on- and off-line. And it's often forgotten that Larry Page and Sergey Brin developed Google's search algorithm by updating PageRank, a method for ranking academic articles they encountered while using the Stanford University library.

"Many of us thought search was a solved problem," Stanford president John Hennessy said as we sat in his sun-splashed office on the Stanford Quad. "AltaVista was out there and did a great job of crawling and presenting information in the order it appeared." But the masses of information it produced were virtually unsorted. "On an AltaVista search," the Stanford president recollected, "I would type *Hennessy*, and the first thing that would pop up would be fifty different sites for Hennessy cognac. That's not the Hennessy I wanted," he said, chuckling. "When Gerhard Casper was Stanford's president, he complained that when he did a search for *Casper* it would come up as Casper the Friendly Ghost. For a German constitutional lawyer, that's not funny." Page and Brin, students at the time, realized that the idea behind PageRank could be applied to rank searches online. "Google was based on reapplying existing technology," Hennessy explained. "It took a couple of young people that didn't think that search was a solved problem to apply an old technology to the emerging Web."

How do we improve our chances of making Sunbird leaps? Being flexible enough to consider information that seems irrelevant is an important first step. Sunbirds actively play with analogies and continually ask how existing knowledge might be repurposed. Thinking back to a similar situation in the past often pushes ideas forward. Sunbirds evaluate how and why a strategy worked in the first place and what it will take to translate it to a new arena.

Instead of trying to invent a new heart stent, imagine a helicopter blade; instead of developing a new way to deliver drugs, consider an Intel chip; instead of making ordinary instant coffee, transport freeze-dried medical technology to maintain coffee's distinctive flavor. To get a better sense of how Sunbirds think, consider the following problem:

> Suppose you are a doctor faced with a patient who has a malignant tumor in his stomach. It is impossible to operate, but unless the tumor is destroyed, the patient will die. There is a kind of ray that can be used to destroy the tumor. If the rays reach the tumor all at once at a sufficiently high intensity, the tumor will be destroyed. Unfortunately, at this intensity, the healthy tissue that the rays pass through on the way to the tumor also will be destroyed. At lower intensities, the rays are harmless to healthy tissue, but they will not affect the tumor either. What type of procedure might be used to destroy the tumor with the rays, and at the same time avoid destroying the healthy tissue?

When Mary Gick and Keith Holyoak of the University of Michigan posed this problem as part of a cognitive psychology experiment, less than 10 percent of participants could find a solution. However, there is a way to increase the chances of saving the patient. It involves thinking through a seemingly unrelated story:

> A small country was ruled from a strong fortress by a dictator. The fortress was situated in the middle of the country, surrounded by farms and villages. Many roads led to the fortress through the countryside. A rebel general vowed to capture the fortress. The general knew that an attack by his entire army would capture the fortress. He gathered his army at the head of one of the roads, ready to launch a full-scale direct attack. However, the general then learned that

the dictator had planted mines on each of the roads. The mines were set so that small bodies of men could pass over them safely, since the dictator needed to move his troops and workers to and from the fortress. However, any large force would detonate the mines. Not only would this blow up the road, but it would also destroy many neighboring villages. It therefore seemed impossible to capture the fortress.

The general devised a simple plan. He divided his army into small groups and dispatched each group to the head of a different road. When all was ready, he gave the signal, and each group marched down a different road. Each group continued down its road to the fortress so that the entire army arrived at the fortress at the same time. In this way, the general captured the fortress and overthrew the dictator.

When participants were told the story of the fortress before they were presented with the tumor problem, approximately 75 percent figured out how to save the patient. They were able to transport insight gained in a military scenario and apply it to a medical situation. They could see a way for the doctor to divide radiation into smaller doses administered from different angles that would strike the tumor with enough intensity to destroy it while preserving surrounding tissue. Normally, people who are presented with the problem of the patient with stomach cancer fixate on the tumor and the radiation protocol. They conclude that the patient won't survive. But when we allow our minds to search for different analogies, alternative approaches can emerge.

Sunbirds willingly look in places that others dismiss. They gain an advantage from knowing a little bit about a lot of things and repurpose knowledge from seemingly unrelated fields.

It would be a mistake, however, to think that importing and exporting ideas, as Sunbirds do, is the only way to spot opportunity. Some creators build novel solutions from the bottom up.

ARCHITECTS: BUILDING NEW MODELS FROM THE GROUND UP

In 2001, Elon Musk and his friend Adeo Ressi, who had been a housemate at Penn, were stuck in slow-moving traffic on the Long Island Expressway. They began brainstorming about what to do next with their careers. Both were successful entrepreneurs. Ressi had started the software development company Methodfive and Musk's company PayPal was about to go public. As they drove, their conversation turned to interplanetary space exploration. What could one person do to make it possible? At first, they dismissed the question as a joke. Space travel, they agreed, was too expensive, too complicated. But as they inched along in traffic, they wondered: How difficult could it be? As they drove a few miles farther, they attempted to calculate how much spacecraft cost. They broke space travel down into its component parts and debated the elements. As they approached the Midtown Tunnel into Manhattan, they were beginning to wonder when NASA planned to go to Mars.

Musk went straight to his computer to check the NASA Web site for information on plans for a NASA Mars mission. But he found no schedule. Why? "I expected to find that we were well on our way, but there was no information," he said. One of the things Musk wanted to do with his newfound wealth was to reinvigorate interest in space, so he decided to underwrite an experiment to see if plants from Earth could grow in Mars's soil. Musk envisioned sending a small greenhouse to the Martian surface in which plants would be fed by a rehydrated nutrient gel. He would call the greenhouse the Mars Oasis. "You'd have this cool shot of green plants on a red planet to get people really fired up," Musk said enthusiastically. Yet in evaluating the various components required to make this happen, he encountered a problem: "I could compress the costs of everything else, but I got stuck with the cost of the rocket."

He traveled to Russia to explore buying refurbished intercontinental ballistic missiles. Though he negotiated a price of $20 million each, much cheaper than the $65 million per rocket in the United States, Musk still found the cost prohibitive.

Wondering whether it was possible to create a more advanced rocket that could dramatically lower the cost of access to space, Musk recruited aerospace engineer and business startup consultant Jim Cantrell and tracked down Tom Mueller, a propulsion engineer who lived on the edge of the Mojave Desert. Mueller had built a rocket engine in his garage. Working with Cantrell and Mueller, Musk assembled a team to do a feasibility study to determine if a cheaper launch vehicle could be built. It became clear that nothing material stood in the way. "I think we can build it ourselves," Musk asserted.

REASONING BY FIRST PRINCIPLES

What makes someone an Architect? These creators identify openings, and, as blank-sheet-of-paper builders, they construct solutions from the ground up. Just like professional architects who design skyscrapers, they have a unique ability to see vacancies and envision how separate parts can fit together to form a new logical design.

Architects start by looking for what is *not* there. Instead of focusing on existing solutions, they hunt for what is missing. They listen for silence and pay attention to what others ignore. When they detect the slightest anomaly, Architects ask "Why?" Many of us pick up on anomalies or gaps but tend to fit discrepancies into existing frames of reference. Architects don't dismiss inconsistencies. They seize upon what they detect.

Musk wondered why existing rockets were so expensive and began to examine the situation. The problem, as he conceived it, was that they were developed for maximum performance without regard to cost. Almost without exception, rockets were made to order and could not be used more than once. If every Boeing 747 were thrown away after a single flight from New York to London, air travel would be prohibitively expensive, too. Musk reasoned that reusability was the crux of the problem. In addition, governments purchased rockets on a cost-plus basis from large aerospace companies that sought to avoid risk. Boeing, Raytheon, Lockheed Martin, and others used components in rockets developed in the 1960s that were manufactured by subcontractors, further increasing costs and complexity. "We needed a new company to create a forcing function for technological improvement, so that's why I started SpaceX," Musk said.

Architects unpack assumptions and test different variables to order new solutions. They believe rigorous questioning is the hallmark of discovery, and they retain a certain childlike naïveté, a beginner's mind. They ask of all assumptions, "Can this be done differently?"

Musk started by asking, "What's a rocket made of?" Aerospace-grade aluminum alloys, titanium, copper, carbon fiber, among other materials. What's the value of those materials on the commodity market? It turned out that the cost of the materials in a rocket was less than 2 percent of the typical price. This convinced him he could make a much cheaper rocket. Using Tom Mueller's garage-designed Merlin engine, Musk began to build a launch vehicle piece by piece. When a vendor told him that making a smaller valve would cost a quarter of a million dollars and take a year, Musk started manufacturing the valve in house. When a different vendor increased the price of the aluminum domes that top off fuel tanks, Musk started a dome manufacturing facility at the back of SpaceX's Hawthorne, California, factory. Today, SpaceX manufactures 80 percent of the parts for its rockets in house, one at a time.

"When I started SpaceX, I had never made any physical thing before," Musk told me. "I didn't really know how large physical objects were made." But he boiled things down to fundamental truths and reasoned from there. "I tend to approach things from a first principles framework," he explained.

First principles are fundamental elements upon which a theory is based. In mathematics, they are postulates or axioms, whereas in physics a calculation is said to be "from first principles" if it builds up from elemental truths. In philosophy, first principles are defined as foundational assumptions; Aristotle describes them as origins upon which a system is based. Reasoning by first principles requires that gap-seeking Architects identify assumptions one by one and understand what is challenging about each element.

Forging a new path requires fortitude, often without validation. "We did have a lot of issues, for sure," Musk admitted. On March 24, 2006, at a testing ground in the Marshall Islands, he attempted his first rocket launch. Just after liftoff, a fuel leak touched off a fire in the engine. The rocket plummeted. One year later, an oscillating motion caused a second failure. On August 3, 2008, a third rocket fell into the sea, taking with it a NASA-contracted payload and the ashes of actor James Doohan, who had played Scotty on the original *Star Trek* TV series. "It was very stressful. Quite awful, actually," Musk recalled. John Glenn, the first American to orbit the Earth, publicly criticized Musk's efforts to commercialize space. Musk had spent $100 million of his fortune and had to raise outside capital to attempt another launch. Yet four days after the third crash, Musk wrote on the SpaceX blog that he was "certain as to the origin of this problem."

Three. Two. One. Liftoff. Orange flames and brilliantly lit clouds of smoke erupt around a twenty-two-story rocket as 1.3 million pounds of thrust push it into the night sky. Atop the rocket is Dragon, a space-going cargo vessel that will soon rendezvous with the International Space Station, bringing its crew fresh supplies of food and clothing, plus some new science experiments. Applause breaks out in the control tower at NASA's Cape Canaveral as it becomes clear that the launch is a success. But it isn't NASA engineers or leaders of the military-industrial complex doing high-fives. Wearing khaki shorts and T-shirts, the small group crowded into the control tower is led by Elon Musk. The date: May 22, 2012.

Nine days later, on May 31, 2012, having made history as the first privately designed, built, and launched spacecraft to resupply the International Space Station—Dragon separates from the station and begins its reentry into Earth's atmosphere.

"Splashdown successful!!" Musk announces via Twitter as the spacecraft completes its mission—two minutes ahead of schedule.

Today, SpaceX holds more than $1.6 billion in contracts from NASA to resupply the International Space Station, has 36 launches on order, and employs 3,000 people who design and build rocket engines.

Musk succeeded in developing a series of next-generation rockets that can deliver payload-bearing capsules to space at a fraction of the cost of rockets developed by national space programs such as NASA and the European Space Agency. A self-taught engineer, Musk has built a rocket and capsule that cost roughly one-tenth as much to launch as the space shuttle.

Musk's larger objective, however, is to make life multiplanetary. After a quick, head-spinning review of billions of years of evolutionary history, he told me that taking life to Mars is the next step in evolution. This will only be possible with much lower costs, and that will require building reusable technology. "Now we're starting to do the first tests of the vertical takeoff and landing version of the rocket," Musk said, with delight in his eye. "Kind of like in sci-fi movies—the rocket takes off and lands on a sheet of flame. That's how a rocket *should* work."

Architects are *problem finders*. They identify friction points, bottlenecks, and complications, and craft new solutions.

A year after starting SpaceX, Musk watched as General Motors did a mandatory recall of the Electric Vehicle 1 from its customers (all of whom were leasers), then crushed the cars. EV1 drivers held candlelight vigils. "That's when I thought there was a need to create Tesla," Musk said, "to spur the industry back toward creation of sustainable transport."

Just as he broke down the fundamental parts of a rocket to see how one could be reassembled more cheaply, Musk analyzed the components of batteries, measured cost, and used first principles to build a new kind of all-electric vehicle. Despite the fact that battery power costs about $600 per kilowatt hour, he assessed the spot market value of carbon, nickel, aluminum, and steel on the London Metal Exchange. He totaled up the cost of these principal components of a battery pack and concluded that the combined price could be much closer to $80 per kilowatt hour. Musk believes that battery-powered vehicles will continue to increase in performance capacity and decrease in cost.

In 2006, Musk noted that high costs prevented the average

American homeowner from installing rooftop solar panels. He identified a need to consolidate distribution of solar panel installation and started SolarCity with his cousins Lyndon and Peter Rive. SolarCity designs, installs, and monitors solar panels, and it partners with banks and large companies to offer financing. Consumers gain a return on their investment by realizing continued savings on heating costs.

"Where's the pain?" Architects ask, believing that once you identify a problem, you're on the way to solving it. Challenges can be as cosmic as Elon Musk's quest to "solve problems of humanity"—or as practical as making undergarments more comfortable. Architects uncover opportunity by staying alert to irritations—such as one that was *really* getting on Sara Blakely's nerves.

Selling fax machines door to door in Atlanta, Sara Blakely spent a lot of her workday walking from office to office in the Georgia heat. In order to look professional, Blakely wore panty hose under her pants. She liked the way the nylons smoothed her figure, but she hated the discomfort. And the seams stuck out from her open-toed kitten heels. To remedy the problem, she cut the feet out of her panty hose, but that didn't work because the nylon inched up her legs.

She went to department stores to ask what she could wear under her slacks. "They kept bringing me to the shaper department and showing me these huge, thick biker shorts with big bands," Blakely recalled. There was absolutely no way that would work under white pants. Others suggested wearing a thong. "Well, that isn't going to help with my cellulite. I still feel a bit insecure in these pants, wearing a thong," she protested. What did other women do? Blakely said a sales associate at Neiman Marcus told her, "A lot of women are already cutting the feet out of their panty hose and using rubber bands to tie them down." That was proof enough for Blakely. "I saw it for what it was," she said. "An opportunity!"

Blakely had never taken a business class or worked in fashion merchandising. Her major at Florida State was legal communications, but she said she "bombed the LSAT" twice. Before selling fax machines, she worked at Walt Disney World, where she wore a brown polyester suit and helped load people from a moving sidewalk onto rides.

Yet Blakely always reasoned independently. She set out to make a homemade prototype of footless panty hose and began cold-calling hosiery mills. Nobody would listen. "I had to go face-to-face," Blakely told me. "So I took a week off work and drove to North Carolina to meet all the people who hung up on me, to beg them in person. And that's when I realized *they were all men.*"

She tried to explain her footless panty hose idea and why she wanted to use hosiery material for a shaper. They didn't get it. Then it dawned on her: "Maybe that's why panty hose are so uncomfortable!" The people making panty hose aren't the people wearing them. "Do you know how miserable we are?" Blakely asked the male manufacturers. "We're cutting our waistbands at lunch. We're splitting them. We can't breathe."

Touring the mills, she began to break down the problem. Manufacturers put an average-size waistband on all products to cut costs. Sizes small and extra large were made with the same elastic waist. To test products, she said, men stood with clipboards staring at plastic forms, saying: "Yup, that's a medium." Women never tried on the panty hose.

Despite talking with suppliers face-to-face during her trip to the Tar Heel State, Blakely met with rejection. But two weeks later, she got a call. The manager of a Highland Mills hosiery factory said,

"Sara, I've decided to make your crazy idea." His three daughters had convinced him over dinner, saying, "Dad, that's a really smart idea. You should help this girl."

Architects relentlessly press forward, often without outside validation. For the first year, Blakely shared her idea only with manufacturers and lawyers who could help her move it forward. "Most of us want to tell our coworkers or friends, or husbands and wives, our ideas, for what reason? We want them to say, 'Yes, that is a good idea.' We want validation. But I feel that ideas are the most vulnerable in their infancy," Blakely said. "Out of love and concern, friends and family give all the reasons or objections on why they shouldn't do it. I didn't want to risk that." Building new concepts takes time, and reframing a problem requires fortitude.

"Kind of the way somebody else gets a huge high if they hit a home run, it was a huge high for me to figure out a better way to make something," Blakely told me. "But it took an insane amount of fire in the belly to do it my own way."

Blakely wanted to patent her idea. She visited several top law firms in Atlanta to explain her product to audiences of men. It became evident that they had a difficult time grasping the potential of her invention. One attorney kept looking nervously about the room; he later admitted he thought her idea was a prank and that he was being secretly filmed for a reality TV show. For a fee of $3,000, she could get help writing the patent. Considering the fee exorbitant, she bought a book to learn how to write the patent herself. She enlisted her mother, a watercolor artist, to sketch the product design, and found a lawyer who, for $700, would write in a single legal clause she needed. Blakely heard that the "k" sound in products, such as Coca-Cola and Kodak, caught consumers' attention. One day while driving, it hit her: she would name the product Spanks. She later changed it to Spanx to make the trademark more recognizable.

Confidence often comes from being shown how to do something and then mastering it, but Architects build new products without anyone showing them how. They believe they might have a better way, and press forward without a need for affirmation.

"Lucky for me, no one showed me how to do a business," Blakely said. For example, she landed the Neiman Marcus account simply by calling and convincing a buyer to meet her for ten minutes. To demonstrate the problem and her solution, Blakely led the buyer into the ladies' room, ducked into a stall, and appeared moments later wearing Spanx under her white pants. Later, people asked, "How did you ever land Neiman Marcus?" The industry norm is to demonstrate products at trade shows. "I called," Blakely said with a smile. At the time, she didn't know that trade shows existed.

"Today, I ask employees, 'If you didn't know how your job was done, how would you be doing it?'" Blakely told me. "Just take fifteen minutes. Wipe everything you know clean. How would you do this if no one else showed you how to get it done?" As an example, she explained how a new kind of bra would be developed: "I just see a bra and I think, 'Why is the bra the way it is? Why did they create it that way to begin with? Because that was all the technology available? How could it be more comfortable, and does it make sense that there's two elastic bands that go across our back that pinch our skin? How can we rethink it?'" The Spanx Bra-llelujah bra, which has become a best seller, was created by asking those questions. Architects take an everyday item and ask, "Why is it that way?" and "What can make it better?"

Everyone, from Julia Roberts to Gwyneth Paltrow to Jessica Alba to next-door neighbors and cubicle mates, raves about Spanx: the body-smoothing undergarments have become a word-of-mouth sensation. By 2012, Spanx's Footless Pantyhose and Power Panties had sold more than nine million and six million pairs, respectively.

Spanx founder Sara Blakely became the world's youngest self-made female billionaire.

Given Architects' proclivity to deconstruct and reconstruct assumptions to make discoveries, they *think* all the time. "I am a recreational thinker," Blakely said, sitting in her bright red office, one wall of which is papered from floor to ceiling with old *Life* magazine covers. "I don't have hobbies or watch TV. I'm just thinking all the time." In fact, Blakely explained, she builds in a unique way to create time to think before the workday gets started. "I live five minutes from Spanx, but I get in the car forty-five minutes before I have to be at the office and drive a fake commute," she explained. Somehow the activity of driving frees her mind to hatch new ideas. Elon Musk said something similar: "It's just always there in the back of my mind. I'm working things out when I sleep, when I'm in the shower, whenever I'm awake." Jack Dorsey, cofounder of social networking service Twitter and mobile payments company Square, thinks as he walks to and from work in San Francisco. His dual offices and residence are set up to give him time to contemplate ideas.

What do these creators think about? They make better use of anomalies than most of us. They operate somewhat like a detective trained to notice inconsistencies in case materials, discrepancies in testimony, or glitches in a sequence of events. We know when something isn't quite right. We experience "tacit awareness," as academics call it, when we detect an inconsistency, yet most people dismiss that perception. Architects, by contrast, run with it, asking questions like these: Might there be an obscure detail that can open a different angle? Might there be another way to understand the situation? What strategies have others abandoned?

Architects remain open to figuring out another way to conceive of an original solution. The work of creativity scholar Jacob Getzels supports the notion that some people aren't locked into preconceived notions of what a challenge means. The following example helps to illustrate the importance of what academics call "problem-finding":

An automobile is traveling on a deserted country road and blows a tire. The occupants of the automobile go to the trunk and discover there is no jack. They define their dilemma by posing the problem: "Where can we get a jack?" They look about, see empty barns but no habitation. They recall that several miles back they had passed a service station. They decide to walk back to the station to get a jack.

While they are gone, an automobile coming from the other direction also blows a tire. The occupants of this automobile go to the trunk and discover there is no jack. They define their dilemma by posing the problem: "How can we raise the automobile?" They look around and see, adjacent to the road, a barn with a pulley for lifting bales of hay to the loft. They move the automobile to the barn, raise it on the pulley, change the tire, and drive off.

How the problem is defined will determine what solutions might be discovered. "I like to think of things as broadly as possible," Elon Musk explained. "When I see a problem, I just start asking questions," Sara Blakely said. "I am looking for a gap." By taking a step back, these creators give themselves space to consider alternatives.

Architects strip away layers of preconceived notions. They deconstruct and reconstruct assumptions, building ideas from the bottom up.

But there is also a select group of creators with the ability to meld solutions from a variety of sources to build hybrid outcomes. I call them Integrators.

INTEGRATORS: COMBINING CONCEPTS

"I want BOTH!" Steve Ells, founder of Chipotle, the $3.6-billion-a-year chain of fast-casual Mexican restaurants, said when we met at the company's New York City office. "I was never a good compromiser, even as a little kid. My parents would offer me a choice, and I would answer, 'I want both!' I guess it's just the way I think."

Growing up in Boulder, Colorado, Ells would sit glued in front of the television—not watching Mickey Mouse or Bugs Bunny, but *The Galloping Gourmet* and Julia Child. When just a grade schooler, he learned how to make hollandaise sauce; when he was in high school, he began collecting cookbooks and hosting dinner parties. At the University of Colorado, "everyone was broke, and Steve would make duck confit with a wine reduction sauce," recalls Monty Moran, a friend, now co-CEO of Chipotle. "He'd use the most expensive butter he could find, and the best salt. He found a way to spend more at the grocery store than anyone else in history."

It's no surprise that after graduating from college, Ells enrolled at the Culinary Institute of America, in Hyde Park, New York. "It was really, really fun. I had a blast," he recollected, his voice full of enthusiasm. He then moved to San Francisco to work with celebrity chef Jeremiah Tower at Stars restaurant.

On his days off, Ells headed to San Francisco's Mission District, where the spices, aromas, and flavors of Mexican cuisine captivated him. One day at a taqueria, he watched the line of customers grow until it wound out the door and around the corner. The wait was worth it: the food was fresh, hot, and satisfying. Ells grabbed a napkin and noted the number of people in the line and how quickly it moved, estimated the average check, then did some calculations. The taqueria was a cash cow.

Ells excitedly telephoned his father, a pharmaceutical executive. "Slow down, Steve," his dad said. "You want to sling burritos?" That he did.

Two weeks later, Ells packed a U-Haul truck, drove back to Colorado, and signed a lease for his first restaurant. "I paid $750 a month for an 850-square-foot spot. I hired a haphazard contractor and saved money by going to the hardware store and picking up inexpensive raw materials that I thought would look cool," he said.

The first Chipotle launched in 1993.

Ells aimed to create a fast-food restaurant that would be the antithesis fast food. "I really didn't compromise when I opened Chipotle. I wanted high-quality ingredients, and I wanted to serve them quickly, efficiently, and affordably," he said. By integrating his Culinary Institute–honed skills with the techniques behind Mexican street food, he created a new dining category—fast casual.

Unlike Sunbirds, who transport ideas across divides, or Architects, who build new concepts from the ground up, Integrators combine existing elements to shape novel outcomes. They invent a new way forward by assembling opposites.

Unusual spice combinations yield exotic foods. Fusing retro and modern trends shapes fashion. We laugh at discordant juxtapositions of ideas in jokes. In art, abstract forms such as cubism, made famous by Pablo Picasso and Georges Braque, represent objects broken up and reassembled; in music, jazz emerged from the confluence of African and European traditions. In academics, behavioral economics, bioinformatics, and geophysics represent new fields created by the integration of disciplines.

Yet while combinations strike us as natural once in place, they can be tricky to achieve. Integrators uncover opportunities to overlap ideas and find ways that two disparate elements might make a good marriage.

How do Integrators do it? One way is to mix and match ingredients. Literally.

"We source sustainably raised ingredients; we prepare them according to classic cooking techniques; we serve them in an interactive format that allows customers to get what they want not only for taste, but for diet. It's totally customizable," Chipotle founder Steve Ells explained.

At Chipotle, cooks work in an open kitchen, so everyone can watch. "I wanted people to see we're making our guacamole from whole avocados," Ells said. As a classically trained chef, he did not want Chipotle to compromise on fresh ingredients for convenience or cost. But unlike most professional gourmets, he sought to deliver high-quality food quickly and at an affordable price.

Fast food traditionally has been "order by number," Ells explained with disdain. "You would say 'one,' and someone would turn their back to you and give you a prepacked, highly processed food product." Even today, fast food is highly mechanized. "People aren't cooking," he said. "It's highly, highly processed, designed to be super consistent—and consistently average."

Instead of depending on premade foods to speed service, Ells devised a model he calls "cooking for the service line." Cooks have to watch. As the customer line grows, they increase the amount they prepare, and as the line tapers off, they pull back.

The method accommodates classic cooking techniques. "A lot of things we make take a very extensive prep time," as well as "a very long cook time," Ells said. "But you can prepare in such a way to serve a lot of people quickly and do everything from scratch."

Integrators don't haphazardly meld elements. They don't simply expand categories to add new and different items. They fuse distinct pieces, with a focus on filling a specific gap.

Ells offers just four menu items: burrito, burrito bowl, taco, and salad. Chipotle doesn't sell coffee, cookies, or breakfast. Instead, Ells recombines ingredients with an aim to make the "best burrito in the world."

"I'm always tweaking, always trying to make it better, constantly moving the dials and levers," Ells explained. Recent updates include a different technique for rehydrating chipotles, which are dried and smoked jalapeños, to give them an even smokier taste; dicing onions by hand (food processors remove too much moisture); charring the jalapeños differently; and giving more roasting time to the tomatillos, which are one of the main ingredients in Chipotle's green salsa. Can a customer taste the difference made by any one improvement? Probably not. But taken as a whole, Ells's fast-casual creation appeals to the masses.

"Food with Integrity" is the latest layer Ells has integrated into the mix. In 2001, he visited Niman Ranch and realized that fresh ingredients were not enough. A celebrated ranch and food distributor based near San Francisco, Niman Ranch raises animals with no antibiotics or hormones and supplies high-end restaurants such as Berkeley's Chez Panisse. Organic vegetables and free-range beef, chicken, and pork are typically not found in the fast-food industry. "I think that sustainably raised ingredients should not be an elitist pursuit," Ells told me. "It should be something that everyone is able to have."

The cooking techniques, ingredients, burrito concept, and restaurant style all existed before Chipotle. Yet Steve Ells saw a way to reorder existing elements to create a new fast-casual category. "I started a fast-food restaurant, but I didn't know the fast-food rules," Ells said. "So everything I did was sort of fine-dining centric."

NOVELTY THROUGH INTEGRATION

How do Integrators see possibilities? One way is by evaluating elements independently to decipher how individual pieces might be joined differently.

"The Candle Problem," laid out by Gestalt psychologist Karl Duncker and updated in 2003 by Stanford researchers Michael Frank and Michael Ramscar, provides an example.

In the experiment in its original form, participants are presented with a candle, some matches, and a box of thumbtacks. Using only these items, they are asked to attach the candle to the wall. Most attempt to melt the candle to the wall or attach it with the thumbtacks. Participants discover what works only about 25 percent of the time. The way to complete the task is to empty the box of tacks, tack it to the wall, and use the box as a shelf upon which to put the candle. The trick is to reinterpret the box of tacks as a shelf. Most people don't think of this. They suffer from what academics describe as "functional fixedness."

Yet, when Frank and Ramscar updated the experiment simply by underlining the individual words in the description, "on the table there is a candle, a box of tacks, and a book of matches," the proportion of participants who discovered the solution doubled to about 50 percent. When the researchers highlighted discrete elements, participants were twice as likely to be more creative in seeing what was available to them. It's this kind of ability to see pieces independently that enables Integrators to disentangle elements and assemble them in new and different amalgamations.

Integrators also uncover opportunities by combining contrasting ideas. Merging opposites can yield breakthrough discoveries. Although no one formula exists, novelty through integration is a phenomenon studied by creativity researchers. Thomas Ward, a psychology professor at the University of Alabama, analyzed the processes that uncover new ideas and found that atypical combinations yield the greatest number of emergent properties. In 2002, Ward conducted research in which college students interpreted various types of adjective-noun combinations and were told to "think of a single meaning that best describes the pair." His most notable finding was that unusual combinations, such as "undressed enemy" or "entertaining delay," and pairs of words with opposing meanings, such as "healthy illness" or "painful joy" prompted the most creative responses.

Consider the concept of a "luxury SUV." By combining a high-end vehicle designed for comfort with an all-wheel, off-road sport vehicle built for rugged terrain, automakers created an entirely new category. The same fusion of opposites produced "rugged comfort" in travel packages for the adventurous explorer who enjoys the comforts of home, and "shabby chic" in interior design concepts for individuals who seek casual yet upscale home design. Integrators explore the possibility of combining what may seem dichotomous to discover openings in the market. Considering such opposite-meaning words as *excitement* and *tranquility, solitude* and *companionship,* and *luxury* and *affordability* can enable Integrators to identify gaps.

Janusian thinking is a term used to describe the ability to actively conceive of two or more opposite concepts, ideas, or images simultaneously. Derived from the name of the Roman god Janus, who

45

sports two faces gazing in opposite directions, the term was coined by Albert Rothenberg, a psychiatrist and researcher of the creative process. Studying the capacity of Nobel laureates to juxtapose ideas, Rothenberg found that physiologists, chemists, and physicists, as well as Pulitzer Prize–winning writers and other artists, had the ability to conceive integrative ideas by finding a connection between disparate concepts. He postulated that conceptual contradiction can lead to creative results.

This Janusian approach is the hallmark of the founders of Gilt Groupe, an online luxury retailer that has brought together invitation-only sample sales and the mass-market reach of the Web to build a new consumer category called "accessible luxury."

Alexis Maybank and Alexandra Wilkis Wilson dropped everything to shop designer, invitation-only sample sales, rain or shine, in New York City. They would sneak out of their day jobs to dash around Manhattan and buy coveted products at great prices. They knew that sample sales attracted a stampede of in-the-know buyers. Fashionistas nearly fought over racks of clothes to snatch discounts on luxury apparel.

"In 2007, although luxury fashion and e-commerce were separately booming, the two worlds had yet to come together in an exciting way," Maybank said. She previously had helped launch eBay Canada and eBay Motors, and her friend Wilson worked for Louis Vuitton and Bulgari. Given their experience, they saw the intersection of fashion and technology as an opportunity. There was a gap, and they set out to fill it.

"We created the excitement of appointment shopping, limited-time-only and designer friendly, to give our members access to specific items that they otherwise might not have had access to," Wilson said when we met at their fashion-forward headquarters in Manhattan. With three other cofounders, Kevin Ryan, Mike Bryzek, and Phong Nguyen, they built an exclusive, members-only Web site that launched from a closet-size Brooklyn warehouse and grew into a $1 billion business in just five years.

To integrate luxury with the world of online shopping, the Gilt founders built a site offering large, glossy images of apparel being worn by high-end models. The founders wanted consumers to feel as if they were flipping through the pages of a fashion magazine. Part of Gilt's pitch to luxury brands was that it was fresh and fashion-forward, the opposite of the boring Web sites of traditional department stores.

"But those early pitches were no cakewalk at all," Maybank recalled. "Alexandra was going into showrooms that didn't have Wi-Fi, but beyond that, the brands were scared of the word 'Internet,' didn't have a Web site, and were not thinking about how they would go about so-called e-commerce." In 2007, luxury brands needed an education in e-commerce and how it not only could enhance their brand but also reach the customers they sought.

With a background in fashion, Wilson knew how luxury brands would resist the Internet. "Convincing designers to sell their most precious possessions—their merchandise—online and at a discount took having many doors slammed in our faces and ultimately not taking no for an answer," she said.

In November 2007, Gilt's site went live. A thirty-six-hour flash sale ignited competitive fire in shoppers. They grabbed deals on luxury brands. The format required that the site not only be pleasing to the eye but easy to navigate. It was a technical challenge for engineers to create an experience that was fast, downloadable, and relatable. Positioning a Prada bag to look appealing required multiple angles, sophisticated lighting, and a detailed product description, including dimensions. And all items, prices, and descriptions had to be updated twenty-four hours later. Gilt operated as a department store—one that changed merchandise daily.

"Scaling the business could create a shock to the system when 400,000 customers flocked to the virtual doors in the same nanosecond," Maybank said. It would have been impossible to welcome that stampede of customers through actual doors. Because 70 percent of Gilt's sales are made no later than ninety minutes after noon, Eastern time, when the flash sale goes live each day, engineers essentially had to create a platform with nearly the scope of an Amazon.com.

"We were hiring merchandising and fashion people from *Vogue* and *InStyle* magazines and engineers from MIT and Cal Berkeley," Maybank said. "Each of them alone had never interfaced with the other. We worked hard to ensure there were no divas creeping in." From Red Bull addicts wearing noise-canceling headphones in the engineering department to Starbucks latte–sipping fashionistas obsessed with merchandising trends, the Gilt Groupe founders integrated backgrounds to build a business at this unique intersection. Through the process they learned that opposites do, in fact, attract. "Gilt's engineers had better luck recruiting new programmers on days when the company held fashion shoots with models walking around in five-inch heels," Wilson said with a laugh.

Gilt didn't just create a new way of selling luxury goods, it created a new kind of customer who had never bought luxury items before. For many shoppers, Gilt made buying a designer dress or fine handbag a first-time purchase that became addictive.

THE ITCH OF CURIOSITY

The creator's most important tool is curiosity. Bold and incisive inquiry sharpens the mind and senses and leads to unexpected discoveries, fresh opportunities, and aha! moments.

Sunbirds, Architects, and Integrators all ask a myriad of questions. They don't lose their natural curiosity. Preschool children ask nearly a hundred questions a day. As we grow older, though, many of us become less inquisitive. Making the effort to ask questions can sharpen our alertness to opportunities. "You don't invent the answers, you reveal them by finding the right question," explained Jonas Salk, discoverer of the polio vaccine.

Gap-seeking creators raise these questions: What surprises me? What am I missing? How can I remove the impediments? What paradoxes do I see?

Chipotle's Steve Ells explained, "I go out to farms and ask a lot of questions." Spanx's Sara Blakely said, "I asked myself if cutting the feet out of my pantyhose could be the answer. I found it wasn't." For Alexis Maybank of Gilt, a crucial question was, "How could women in Ohio shop sample sales in New York?"

Thinking like a Sunbird, Architect, or Integrator is like strengthening a mental muscle: Your ability to spot an opportunity grows as you practice and engage. It all begins with an alert and questioning mind.

Chapter 2

DRIVE FOR DAYLIGHT

Never look back unless you are planning to go that way.

—Henry David Thoreau

Race-car drivers say that the trick to managing speed at 200 miles per hour is to drive for daylight. They go too fast to navigate by the lines on the pavement or the position of their fellow drivers. Instead, they focus on the horizon and, at high speeds, their hands follow their eyes.

Creators do the same. They navigate around immediate obstacles by keeping their long-term mission in mind. They execute in the moment with laser-like focus, building a product that fits the market and fulfills a need. Hands on the wheel, creators don't benchmark themselves against the competition or focus on industry norms.

They guide their actions with specific maneuvers: they set their sights on the horizon, scan the edges, and avoid nostalgia. In this chapter, we will examine how creators set the pace in a fast-moving global marketplace.

FOCUS ON THE HORIZON

From zero to $1 billion in revenue in five years: that kind of growth is rare, even in Silicon Valley, but Hamdi Ulukaya achieved it in the yogurt business.

Originally from the province of Erzincan, in northeastern Turkey, Ulukaya came to the United States in 1994. He settled in New York City to study English and business, but soon felt out of place. A self-described "dairy boy," he relocated to upstate New York to work on a farm and take classes at the State University of New York at Albany. Ulukaya, who had grown up in rural Turkey, felt more comfortable in the country. His father, on a visit, complained about the mediocrity of American cheeses. "You should make cheese—good cheese," his father insisted. At first Ulukaya balked. He hadn't moved to the United States to do what his family had done back home. But in 2002, Ulukaya changed his mind. He started making feta cheese in a small building in Johnstown, New York. He branded the cheese "Euphrates" and sold it to restaurants and food distributors.

One day, Ulukaya stumbled across a flyer advertising a fully equipped yogurt plant. Thinking it junk mail, he trashed it. But "about half an hour later, with dirt on it, I picked the flyer out of the garbage can," he recalled. "Kraft Foods was shuttering a plant. I called out of curiosity." He drove to South Edmeston, a small town 200 miles north of New York City, to examine the eighty-four-year-old factory. Water was dripping from the ceiling, paint was peeling from the walls, and the outdated equipment was moldering. Nonetheless, Ulukaya wanted to buy the place.

Friends discouraged him. Ulukaya had only a few thousand dollars in the bank, not enough to buy a house, yet he wanted to purchase a decaying yogurt plant. There were a million reasons *not* to buy the factory. Why would an industry stalwart close a plant if it had any value? No matter. Ulukaya set out to make a high-protein, low-fat, Greek-style yogurt that would be superior to anything available in the United States.

American yogurt, Ulukaya said, is too thin, too sweet, and full of preservatives and dyes. It's not *real*. In Turkey, yogurt is a culinary staple, and Ulukaya had grown up eating the thick, tangy variety his mother made on the family farm.

He made decisions with an eye toward the future. With no advertising budget or brand recognition, and knowing his yogurt would be placed on the bottom shelf, Ulukaya designed bold packaging that consumers couldn't miss. His yogurt cup was rounder, shorter, and more substantial. He designed shrink-wrapped sleeves with brightly colored labels, and he printed his logo on the top of the cup so that customers could see the brand when looking down into the case.

"Some days you're smiling and thinking you're going to make this thing rock," Ulukaya said. "Then, the next day, a pipe breaks, the yogurt doesn't taste right, and your costs look too high. As a founder, you have to learn to keep your eyes on an ultimate goal. If you lose sight of that goal, you have to get out. I always saw the goal. It was always there in my head."

In October 2007, Ulukaya and his staff packed the first order of Chobani: 300 cases of strawberry, peach, and blueberry Greek yogurt for a retailer on Long Island. Ulukaya waited an anxious week before asking the store manager how his product had fared.

The yogurt had sold quickly, the manager told him. Chobani was a hit.

Ulukaya wasted no time approaching the ShopRite supermarket chain, which had more than 200 locations, primarily in the Northeast. Because Chobani couldn't afford the high fees major retailers charge to allocate shelf space, he struck deals to deduct fees from Chobani's sales, promising that if the yogurt didn't sell, he would buy back the remaining cups. It worked.

A bigger break came in 2009, when Stop & Shop, Publix, BJ's Wholesale Club, and Costco began to stock Chobani. Demand increased to 400,000 cases per week. One big-box chain suggested that Chobani offer different flavors; without the necessary machinery, Chobani employees assembled orders by hand, just as they had done two years earlier when Ulukaya won his first order.

The company was manufacturing up to half a million cases a week when it reached a crossroads. Knowing that industry leaders such as Dannon and Yoplait would come after a fast-growing startup, Ulukaya pushed weekly production to a million cases. Chobani had to be aggressive, he had determined, to avoid being crushed by bigger competitors.

"Chobani speed" became the mantra. In 2008, the upstate New York plant was producing 15,000 cases of yogurt per week. By early 2011, the same facility was churning out 1.2 million cases. By 2012, the total was 1.8 million. Employing 1,300 workers across multiple production lines operating twenty hours per day, the South Edmeston factory added a fourth shift to keep pace with demand. In 2012, Ulukaya built a second plant in Twin Falls, Idaho, to further ramp up capacity.

When Ulukaya started his business, Greek yogurt accounted for just 0.2 percent of the $78 billion yogurt market in the United States.

At the end of 2013, it accounted for about 50 percent, and Chobani became the top-selling Greek yogurt. "While we've been fortunate to achieve great things, the yogurt story in this country is just beginning," he said.

Every creator revealed the same determination: each wanted to build something extraordinary. To describe how they managed speed and complexity, creators turned to auto racing analogies.

- "I call it driving to success," said Gilman Louie, founder of CIA venture capital arm In-Q-Tel and the investment firm Alsop Louie Partners. "Entrepreneurs are always looking for daylight. Their business model acts like a race-car driver's hands. It's always being adjusted."
- "There's gears, belts, valves, tubes—everything's connected, and it all has to work together," explained Joe Gebbia, Airbnb cofounder. Describing the company's explosive growth, he said, "The gears started to touch, they started to move, people started using the service, and we started driving forward. We've never looked back."
- "You've always got to be able to look forward and drive forward," Kevin Plank said about Under Armour. "You've got to dictate the tempo."

To harness momentum, auto racers accelerate out of turns, grip straightaways, and "drive through the windshield." They execute their vision, staying aware of other drivers but focusing on their own trajectory. Creators move with similar precision.

MAP THE ROAD AHEAD

"You have to have clarity on why you are doing something, what motivates you, and how to deal with things that are really difficult," Theranos founder Elizabeth Holmes told me. "If we can apply technology to detect disease in time to do something about it, we can fundamentally shape the way in which prevention becomes possible."

Why is it that cancer often isn't discovered until it has progressed so far that treatment is difficult? Or that heart disease becomes apparent only after someone has had a heart attack? Holmes founded life sciences company Theranos to create a new generation of diagnostic tests that one day will allow physicians and patients to pounce on illness before it spreads and treat conditions before they worsen.

"I wanted to make actionable health information accessible to people at the time it matters most," Holmes said. "That means being able to detect conditions in time to do something about them and provide information to individuals so that they can live healthier lives."

Laboratory data drive 80 percent of clinical decisions, but since the invention of the clinical analyzer in the 1950s, the way the medical profession conducts blood tests has not fundamentally changed. In a hospital, doctor's office, or clinic, a technician applies a tourniquet to your arm, sticks you with a needle, draws blood into tubes, and sends samples to a centralized lab, where they are manually removed by means of a pipette and processed with a centrifuge or mass spectrometer, or mixed with a chemical reagent. Three days to a week later, your doctor receives the results.

The slowness and general inefficiency of diagnostic blood work is target number one for Holmes. She and her team have designed proprietary technology to make diagnostic tests faster, cheaper, and more accurate. Instead of taking days to grow cultures to detect a virus or bacterium, Theranos races ahead by using DNA profiling to identify pathogens. Results are sent electronically to physicians two to four hours after the sample is taken.

Time can be critical in the treatment of even relatively ordinary ailments. Imagine, Holmes said, a woman who complains of lethargy. The physician orders a blood test, and several days later the results indicate severe anemia. But another diagnostic test—and several more days—is needed to determine what type of anemia it is. Meanwhile, the patient is put on a medication. When she returns for a third office visit, she is told she doesn't have anemia after all, but rather an iron deficiency. The problem is solved, but at considerable expense and additional suffering. All of this would be unnecessary with speedier and more accurate testing, Holmes said.

Holmes is intent on eliminating fear and excuses—an estimated 40 to 60 percent of people don't get needed tests—by making blood work more convenient. Theranos's 2013 partnership with Walgreens to deliver on-site laboratory services is a giant step toward making tests available for millions. Seventy-nine million Americans are prediabetic, for example, and more are at risk from chronic maladies such as lung and cardiovascular disease. Yet many people are oblivious. Opening their eyes to their own health risks is just one of the potential benefits of high-tech testing. For seniors with collapsed veins, children who fear needles, and oncology patients who undergo frequent blood tests, a tiny fingerstick that draws just droplets of blood makes lab tests less uncomfortable, less scary.

Remarkably, Theranos charges less than half the standard Medicare and Medicaid reimbursement rates. If all tests were performed at Theranos prices, Holmes has calculated, Medicare and Medicaid would save more than $200 billion over the next decade.

But her ultimate goal is prevention. Holmes uses the example of the prostate-specific antigen (PSA) test for prostate cancer. It's not the concentration of PSA that matters but the rate of change. "If you showed me a single movie frame and asked me the narrative, I wouldn't be able to tell you the story," Holmes explained. "But with many frames, the story unfolds." And Theranos supplements its tests with software that lets doctors and patients see the bigger picture.

"The dream is to be able to help tailor therapy much earlier in the disease progression than has ever been possible," Holmes said. "Right now we are attacking a physical tumor when it's already present. We want to change the way we think about these conditions. With a lot of these things, if you catch them early, you have a better chance to make them right."

TO-GO THINKING

A radically forward-looking approach is key to creators' ability to achieve their goals. Research conducted by University of Chicago psychologists Minjung Koo and Ayelet Fishbach shows that an individual's perspective on his or her own progress has a profound effect on accomplishment. They found that people who are pursuing goals focus on either what remains to be done—"to-go" thinking—or how far they've come already—"to-date" thinking. Although both can increase motivation, researchers say to-go thinking accelerates accomplishment when individuals are committed to a goal.

Here's one way to explain it: You're running a marathon, and you're at mile eighteen. Your heart is pounding, and sweat is pouring down your face. Your knees, ankles, and feet ache with every lunge forward. Your breathing is getting labored. But you remain on course, determined to cross the finish line. How do you stay motivated? Are you thinking of the eighteen miles you have already completed, or are you thinking of the 8.2 miles to go? If your answer is what's to go, then you, like other creators, have the mental framework necessary to succeed.

Koo and Fishbach found that when we are committed to a certain goal, focusing on past accomplishments tempers motivation. However, if we consider what we have left to do, motivation is not only sustained, but quickened. When we do to-go thinking, we compute what we have accomplished and where we want to be. After detecting the difference between the two, we narrow the gap by applying greater concentration and effort.

Koo and Fishbach's research shows that to-go thinking increases motivation by drawing attention to progress yet to be made. In one study, for example, college students preparing for an exam in a core course were divided into two groups. Students in one group were told they had 52 percent of the material left to cover, while students in a second group were reminded that they had already completed 48 percent of the work. Looking forward, the students who were focused on the remaining 52 percent were more motivated than their counterparts who'd been encouraged to think retrospectively. In another example, fundraisers campaigning to raise money to help AIDS orphans in Africa sent solicitation letters to regular donors emphasizing either the to-date condition ("To this point, we have successfully raised $4,920 through various channels") or the to-go condition ("We have successfully raised money through various channels and need another $5,080"). When their attention was drawn to the funds needed to complete the campaign, people who cared about the cause increased their pledge donations. They perceived that progress was not being made quickly enough, and contributed. To-go thinking prompts us to focus on the ground we have left to cover.

Motivating yourself by thinking about how much of the marathon remains before you cross the finish line can inspire you to run harder, faster, more competitively, and with greater enthusiasm. The same applies to the business world. Creators focus on the desired result to gain momentum.

"I'm here to build something for the long term. Anything else is a distraction," Facebook cofounder Mark Zuckerberg said when he declined Yahoo's $1 billion offer to buy his social networking service in 2006. The average twenty-two-year-old would have accepted millions in profit from a dorm-room experiment, but Zuckerberg kept his eyes on the horizon. He initially expanded Facebook's domain from Harvard to other Ivy League schools, then to other universities in the Boston area, and soon after to colleges, high schools, and businesses throughout the country and the world. Ultimately, it was Zuckerberg's what's-next attitude that propelled Facebook out of his college dorm room and into the lives of more than a billion people.

Similarly, Sara Blakely had a "no limit" focus from the earliest days of Spanx. "For the first two years, I was every single department," she told me. "I was the packer, the shipper, the before-and-after butt model, the marketer, the salesperson, and trying to figure out QuickBooks. And the whole time, I was making a checklist: 'Not good at that, really don't like this, can't wait to have somebody else do this because this is not my strength.' I think it's important to be self-aware and visualize your goal in a concrete way."

Nick Woodman, founder of digital camcorder company GoPro, turned the idea of tethering cameras to surfers' wrists into a media revolution, capturing high-definition video from cameras mounted on helmets, snowboards, skateboards, and almost anything else. He obsesses about updating products to stay one step ahead. So do the founders of Fuhu, Robb Fujioka, John Hui, and Steve Hui, makers of the Nabi tablet for children. Committed to developing technology to entertain and educate children, in 2014 the Fuhu founders partnered with DreamWorks Animation to create the DreamTab, a tablet for kids with cartoons, songs, and apps from the DreamWorks library.

Creators build toward where they are going, not where they are. This requires anticipating trends and making investments to set up success. Many leaders move too slowly. Blockbuster, Eastman Kodak, and Borders, for example, lost stronghold markets to more forward-leaning creators.

"Yesterday's home run didn't win today's game; you're only as good as your next hit," Jawbone cofounder Hosain Rahman likes to say. After his company's first success with Bluetooth headsets in 2006, Rahman gave everyone at Jawbone a T-shirt with "Underdog" printed on the front. "When you are an underdog, you are scrapping, trying to find a solution, forced to be more innovative than you would like," Rahman explained. Jawbone's forward focus has led to dominant market share in three product categories.

And Chipotle founder Steve Ells strives to make the "best burrito in the world" tastier every year. He doesn't allow managers to hang awards such as "Best Burrito" or "Best Cheap Eats" on Chipotle walls. "We already won those things," Ells said. "Yes, someone thought we were best burrito, but that's now irrelevant because we need to be better than that."

Creators focus on the horizon. They are never complacent. They move quickly to build the next thing.

"We look to solve fundamental problems to free people from a lot of pain that comes along with technology," Dropbox cofounder Drew Houston told me. Then he added, "We tackle *new problems*."

Dropbox launched in 2007 just as Apple released the iPhone. With the explosive popularity of smartphones and tablets, people have more devices than ever, and thus a need to flexibly access files—documents, spreadsheets, videos, music, and photos—from multiple devices.

Dropbox began as a self-made solution to a personal frustration. In 2006, Houston, a graduate student at MIT, boarded a bus from Boston's South Station to New York and realized that he had left his USB thumb drive at home, an oversight that threatened to leave him idle for a four-hour ride. He stewed over not having his files for work. Then he opened up his laptop and started writing code.

A few months later, Houston partnered with Arash Ferdowsi, an MIT computer science student, to build a company that would offer users access to stored documents via the Web. They secured a spot in the Silicon Valley incubator Y Combinator, moved to San Francisco, cranked out code twenty hours a day in a cramped apartment, and started building a business.

To make files easily accessible in a fast and reliable format with seamless cloud storage on any device, Houston and Ferdowsi needed to solve a complex technical challenge: Dropbox had to work on any device, with any operating system, on any browser, in any country.

"You have to prepare yourself for what's on the horizon," Houston said. Preferring not to have to e-mail files back and forth or carry documents on thumb drives, people sought simplicity. Overflowing in-boxes made life complicated. Houston set out to build an online "home" for people's information.

He anticipated today's increased blurring of lines between personal and professional objectives. Just as people use the same pen to write work memos and grocery lists, the same e-mail account to correspond with colleagues and friends, and the same phone to dial professional associates and family, they can use Dropbox for online storage that meets multiple needs.

But focusing on the horizon isn't easy. It requires moving beyond the familiar.

"Since I was a kid, I've always been happiest when writing code," Houston said. "But what you need to build a company is completely different from what you need as an engineer. You have to really push yourself to the edge of your comfort zone." He described growing pains as he pitched the business, gave presentations, and hired and fired friends. "You build systems of code and algorithms that are beautiful, and systems of people that are like trying to build a pyramid out of Jell-O," Houston said. "But you have to do the best you can, and if you're not having problems, you're probably not going fast enough."

He chuckled as he recalled the scramble to receive Dropbox's first $1 million investment in a Bank of America checking account whose balance at the time was only $60. "Two scruffy kids" who turned an idea into a company valued at $10 billion in just seven years, Houston and Ferdowsi focus on what comes next in building their fast-growing firm.

"My cofounder, Arash, sends e-mails at three in the morning saying, 'This letter should be capitalized or two pixels to the left,'" Houston said. "We sweat all the details to set really high standards." It's not comfortable, but the Dropbox founders press full speed ahead to meet the needs of their users, who numbered more than 300 million in 2014.

"If you start thinking you are good at something, that's often the day you stop trying to be better and open the back door for someone to come after you," Houston told me. "For every Google or Facebook, there are also shining stars overtaken—and that's why we always aim higher. We never feel like we're done."

SCAN THE EDGES

Creators and race-car drivers both need to drive for daylight, but with an important difference. Drivers navigate a fixed course—features don't change from lap to lap—whereas creators move at high speeds through an ever-changing environment. They need to be attuned to what is happening along the periphery that might move mainstream.

"Good entrepreneurs are always looking around the edges to see if there's any signal out there that says an original assumption is aging, becoming obsolete, or losing its appeal," In-Q-Tel founder Gilman Louie said. "It's those little hairs that stand up on the back of your neck. You can't send out a marketing team to conduct quantitative or qualitative surveys, because by the time they identify this moment, it's already too late."

Robin Chase had one of these electric moments in 1999 as she listened to her friend Antje Danielson describe a car-sharing experiment she had witnessed in Germany. Emerging mobile technology held the potential to create an alternative to traditional car ownership, she realized. "This is what the Internet was made for," Chase exclaimed. "And I want it!"

As a forty-two-year-old mother of three sharing a vehicle with her husband in Cambridge, Massachusetts, Chase knew she couldn't always borrow her neighbor's car to go to Costco or take her children to a swim meet. She needed a car, but didn't want the hassle and expense of owning one.

With their children in the same kindergarten class, Chase and Danielson often met for coffee, exchanging ideas. Danielson, a PhD geochemist working at Harvard University, thought car sharing on a large scale could be an environmentally sustainable alternative to owning or renting a vehicle. Chase, with an MBA from MIT's Sloan School of Management, drafted a business plan to share with Glen Urban, then dean of MIT Sloan. He was enthusiastic. "This is really amazing. You should do this three times as big and three times as fast," he said.

If you needed a car in 2000, you could buy, lease, or rent, but the concept of sharing one carried a negative connotation. Still, no one talked about hotels as bed sharing or gyms as treadmill sharing, or restaurants as plate and silverware sharing. They were mainstream. Chase and Danielson believed that car sharing would work, but it needed a catchy name. They called it Zipcar.

Pay-as-you-go driving would enable urbanites to run to the grocery store, take the dog to the vet, go to a baby shower in the suburbs, or pick up a colleague at the airport. Most times, city dwellers needed a car only once or twice a week, but instead of owning a car, they could carry a plastic card in their wallet with an embedded computer chip that would unlock a vehicle when they wanted it. "Are you going after the business segment or the consumer segment?" Chase was asked. "Who doesn't want an easy, convenient car?" she would reply. "I need to have all those kinds of drivers."

It was a nontraditional approach to car use that catered to drivers on the edges of the existing market. "You think of car rental: it's this old industry with the regular everyday guys delivering this boring, unremarkable service. We said, 'No, we can make this a cool, urban, hip thing to do,'" Chase explained. "I don't want to rent a car for a day when I only need it for two hours."

Zipcar launched with three lime-green VW Beetles in Cambridge in 2000. In 2001, Zipcar opened in Washington, DC, and in 2002, "wheels when you want them" arrived in New York City. In 2007, Zipcar merged with Flexcar, a regional competitor, and by 2013 Zipcar had more than 760,000 members, with 10,000 vehicles in more than twenty metropolitan areas and on 300 college campuses. In November 2013, Avis acquired Zipcar for $500 million.

Chase and Danielson helped pioneer the sharing economy, but it required acting quickly to capture an emerging change in consumer attitudes about ownership. Similarly, when Joe Gebbia and Brian Chesky first proposed sharing bedrooms with strangers, people told them that renting rooms to strangers was "weird and strange." The Airbnb founders fought a social stigma about sharing. But having hosted paying guests on air mattresses in their apartment, they knew it could be a positive experience.

A few years ago, the idea of staying at a stranger's apartment in a different city seemed risky. But the proliferation of social networks such as Facebook allows Airbnb owners and renters to identify common friends, or friends of friends. Airbnb relies on ratings and reviews to build trust. Guests review their stays. Hosts can write and read reviews of guests, and vice versa.

"If Act One of the Internet was getting people to use e-mail and Web pages, and Act Two was getting people comfortable with transparent reputation, then Act Three is transferring this activity to the offline world," Joe Gebbia said, describing the next frontier.

In 2009, about 100,000 rooms were booked through Airbnb. By 2010, the Airbnb creators had added professional photography services, online payments, and integration with Facebook. The number of guest nights booked grew to more than 750,000. By 2012, Airbnb had exceeded two million nights booked across the United States and internationally. By 2014, more than twenty-five million guests had stayed in Airbnb accommodations.

Like Zipcar founders Chase and Danielson, Airbnb's Gebbia and Chesky brought an idea from the periphery to a wider marketplace. Airbnb originally intended to accommodate conference-goers who couldn't find hotel space. People interested in nontraditional travel destinations and lower-cost options followed. Today, Airbnb provides access to more than 800,000 listings worldwide, offering accommodations in bedrooms, apartments, and houses, as well as in castles, igloos, tree houses, and yurts.

The Airbnb founders examined the edges to unleash a mainstream explosion. "By using Airbnb, you can go from being an outsider to an insider," Gebbia said, describing how Airbnb users share space and cultural experiences.

Kids who removed the wheels from roller skates and bolted them to a plank invented the skateboard. Black Diamond climbing gear was the brainchild of a mountain climber who made pitons—the spikes climbers hammer into rock to gain a foothold—that he sold from the trunk of his car. Hardcore cyclists built mountain bikes by assembling bikes with fat tires to conquer rugged trails. Updating and revising products on the edges of a market is often how creators spearhead a trend.

These peripheral innovators, or "lead users," live in the future, said Eric von Hippel, professor of innovation at MIT Sloan. For thirty years, von Hippel has pioneered research on those who innovate by developing and also adapting products on the edges of markets.

"We were asked to find out how much innovation ordinary people did to develop and modify and adapt products to their own use over a three-year period of time," von Hippel told me as I examined one of the world's first 3-D printers in his office at MIT. Surveying nearly 1,200 people in the United States, Great Britain, and Japan, von Hippel found that lead users invested twice as much as product development firms by developing new products and also modifying existing products to suit their needs. One man built a device to trim treetops from a fishing rod and a large metal hook. A mother made the hands of a clock different colors to help her children learn how to tell time. A mechanic developed a motor to start his car when the battery failed, and a student reprogrammed his GPS to find objects lost in his house. Many such fixes reveal where the next market may arise.

Individuals facing constraints often improvise to meet their needs, and these solutions then go mainstream. 3M, for example, was searching for effective but affordable new approaches to replace or complement the surgical drapes used to prevent bacteria from spreading during surgery. The company studied surgeons in war zones and medical teams in developing markets to determine how they solved similar problems in the field. 3M also learned from the innovations of veterinarians who had developed effective and cheap means of preventing infections when performing surgery on animals. These lead users provided valuable information that enabled 3M to commercialize entirely new methods of preventing surgical infections. In fact, academic research has documented that lead user–generated innovations have consistently created new product lines for 3M, while traditional, marketing research–based methods led to the development of incremental improvements to existing product lines. As a direct result, sales of 3M products based upon lead user innovations averaged $146 million in revenue after five years, more than eight times the sales of products developed by traditional, incremental means.

Creators scan the edges to identify fringe ideas that might move mainstream—in much the same way that race-car drivers anticipate what might emerge in the wider field of vision. And just as auto racers rarely glance at the rearview mirror for fear of sacrificing the split-second opening ahead, creators steer clear of mental ruts and readily jettison old strategies.

AVOID NOSTALGIA

"If we got kicked out and the board brought in a new CEO, what would that man do?" Andy Grove, president of Intel, asked Gordon Moore, CEO and chairman, in 1985. "A new CEO would get Intel out of the memory chip business," Moore responded. Grove thought for a moment, then replied, "Why shouldn't you and I walk out the door, come back, and do it ourselves?" That's exactly what they did.

"Only the paranoid survive," Andy Grove explained as he told this story to a Stanford Business School class I took some years ago. He described "firing himself" to restart Intel in a different direction. Never one to look back, Grove shut down Intel's memory chip business, even though Intel had pioneered the market. He transformed the company to manufacture microprocessors and proceeded to increase Intel's market capitalization from $4 billion to $197 billion—a fifty-fold increase—making Intel, with 64,000 employees, the world's seventh-largest company.

Creators willingly abandon a legacy, even a powerful one that brought them success. They avoid nostalgia. Whether it's a fond memory or a comfortable approach, they refuse to let history hamper progress.

"Entrepreneurs are less likely to engage in counterfactual thinking," said Robert Baron, professor of entrepreneurship at Oklahoma State University. "While they learn from their mistakes, they are not prone to regret or fret over the past. That's a dangerous thing to do."

Academics who study the cognitive factors that influence some to start new ventures describe counterfactual thinking as imagining what might have been. What might have changed if the product had launched two weeks earlier? What might be different if we had recruited the engineer who joined a competitor? In a study of three groups—entrepreneurs, potential entrepreneurs, and non-entrepreneurs—Baron found that people who had recently started their own business were less likely than others to dwell on the past. They didn't worry about missed opportunities. In fact, Baron found that entrepreneurs experienced less regret and were more willing to admit mistakes to themselves and others.

Creators don't get stuck looking back. They take lessons forward and avoid the trap of regret. They don't expend effort on what has happened. Instead, they spend all of their energy on what they can do next.

"It starts with not having a hangover with the way things used to be," Under Armour founder Kevin Plank said.

When Plank launched his company, people told him his idea would never work. Industry heavyweights dominated, they said, and a T-shirt business that had begun at the University of Maryland would never get beyond the locker room. "Let's read the history," investors told Plank. "I remember that. I tried that." Few bought into his vision. "But no one has your answers for you," Plank said with the intensity of a walk-on fullback unafraid to take on larger opponents. His focus is apparent in his Baltimore office. Whiteboards, three panels across and five panels high, line the walls, displaying these phrases: "Attack," "Progress over Perfection," "Walk with Purpose," "Get Out of the Basement and Do Something about It."

For five years, Plank made and remade the original synthetic Under Armour T-shirt. He added long sleeves. Then he did for bottoms what he had done for tops. He took it another step and made a loose-fitting shirt.

One of Plank's biggest hurdles has been the perception that Under Armour is only an apparel company. In 2006, he relied on Under Armour's football pedigree to convince consumers that Under Armour could manufacture a football cleat. The gambit worked. Within two years, Plank had captured 20 percent of the football cleat market. "Since then, we've been on the march," he said.

In 2008, he adopted the mantra "No loser talk" and refused to let the recession stop him. "There will never be a right time," Plank said. "And for those who say I can't do this now, well, somebody has got to get into the game!" Plank challenged industry giants in the $31 billion international athletic footwear market by launching a cross-training shoe. In 2009, Under Armour broke into the running shoe category, and in 2010 the company launched a basketball shoe.

"The best merchants in the world are not the ones who are predicting what's next; rather it's the ones who are dictating what's next," Plank told me. "So our job is to tell the marketplace, 'This is what your football cleat should look like. This is what your training platform should be. This is your running shoe. Here is how it will work with the technology you use every day.'"

Plank even reversed his "cotton-is-the-enemy" philosophy to manufacture a cotton shirt. From its founding, Under Armour had been the anti-cotton company. When Plank took Under Armour public in 2005, in every meeting with investors he would soak a cotton T-shirt in a bucket of water and slap the wet shirt on a tabletop to prove how cotton weighed down athletes. But when Plank looked into customers' closets in 2011, he found that of every thirty T-shirts, twenty-six were cotton. "Then I looked at myself in the mirror and said, 'I don't really have a problem with cotton, either. I just have a problem with the fact that it doesn't perform today,'" he explained.

He took a risk in changing course—consumers might think he sold out. That wasn't it. He set out to design cotton material that would work like a synthetic to keep moisture away from the body. Collaborating with North Carolina–based Cotton Incorporated, Plank created Charged Cotton, a material that dries five times faster than ordinary cotton.

Always one to look forward, Plank tells his target customers, kids just getting started in sports, "If Adidas is your grandfather's brand, and Nike is your father's brand, then Under Armour is for you." Plank doesn't want to persuade the twenty-five-year-old athlete or forty-year-old sports enthusiast to change brands. Rather, he wants to grow with the next generation.

Under Armour's latest product, the E39 T-shirt, which features a biometric measuring system for the body, has a built-in dashboard similar to a car dashboard that measures performance. Plank's 2013 acquisition of MapMyFitness, a fitness-tracking platform that provides users with tools to map, record, and share their workouts, foreshadows a future of digital training and mobile fitness technology. "We have not yet built our defining product," Plank said.

Creators decide what *not* to do every bit as much as they prioritize what's next. Ruling out distractions eliminates obstacles. Making "don't do" lists helps creators overcome hubris and avoid the retrograde force of nostalgia that can hold people back.

Steve Jobs's return to Apple in 1997 provides an example. He drew a two-by-two grid on a whiteboard with "Consumer" and "Pro" on one axis and "Desktop" and "Portable" on the other. Apple would focus on four great products, he said; all others would be terminated. Jobs avoided diffusing his team's energy. At the annual top-100 managers retreat, Jobs asked Apple leaders, "What are the ten things we should be doing next?" As a top-ten list emerged, Jobs erased the bottom seven. "We can only do three," he decreed. No idea, product, or feature was safe from being cut.

Jobs eliminated distractions and ignored diversions. He sought to unclutter design and build "insanely great" products by making consumer technology simple.

Not only that, Jobs believed it was important to leap ahead whenever Apple landed second. He learned that lesson after a profound miss marred the original iMac. Jobs had built the iMac to manage photos and videos, but it couldn't burn CDs; only PC users could rip, burn, download, and swap their favorite songs. "I felt like a dope," Jobs told biographer Walter Isaacson. In response, Jobs unleashed a trifecta: the iPod, iTunes, and the iTunes store.

And despite the success of the iPod, Jobs worried about what might overtake it: "If we don't cannibalize ourselves, someone else will." He concluded that mobile phones posed the next great threat. What if mobile phone makers added music functionality to handsets? This led to the creation of the iPhone, which cannibalized iPod sales almost by design.

Jobs pushed people to do the impossible, slashing products and ideas. "If something sucks, I tell people to their face. It's my job to be honest," he said. His style was famously intolerant. Anyone who worked with him knew Jobs looked in one direction only: forward.

That's how creators work. They seize the wheel, their eyes focused ahead, weaving around the potholes of naysayers and distractions. They have one objective: success. Nothing will get in their way.

Chapter 3

FLY THE OODA LOOP

The ability to learn faster than your competitors may be the only sustainable competitive advantage.

—Arie de Geus

In the summer of 1998, Max Levchin arrived in Palo Alto behind the wheel of a yellow Ryder rental truck he had driven from Chicago. A recent graduate of the University of Illinois at Urbana-Champaign, Levchin had decided to forgo graduate school and join the westward migration of bright young computer engineers. In Palo Alto, he camped on the floor of a friend's apartment while he looked for a job. One day, Levchin attended a talk given by a young derivatives trader named Peter Thiel, as much to escape the heat as to learn something new. He was one of only six in the audience. Thiel's message intrigued him, and after the talk, Levchin pitched some ideas. Thiel was always looking for new investment opportunities, and Levchin piqued his interest enough that he suggested they meet for breakfast.

"It was a bit like nerds courting each other," Levchin recalled. "We began hanging out to decide if we wanted to work together and amused ourselves with math problems. The challenge was often 'I solved this one—can you do it?'"

Thiel invested in Levchin's cryptology concept, and when Levchin couldn't find a CEO, Thiel joined him. They founded Field-Link, a company that encrypted software for Palm Pilots, the now primitive-seeming personal digital assistants that were all the rage at the time. The mathematically complex product failed. They went on to design cryptology software for the enterprise market. Another flop. Undeterred, they devised a "virtual wallet," a secure program that held financial information. It floundered. Next they created an "enforceable IOU" for financial transactions using the Palm Pilot. But no one was interested in mere promises of future payment. Then Thiel and Levchin hit on a winning idea. They relaunched FieldLink as Confinity and introduced a means to beam money instantly and wirelessly between PalmPilot devices. In the summer of 1999, Thiel and Levchin staged a media event at Buck's Restaurant, a famous venture-capital hangout in Woodside, California, to announce Confinity's first round of funding. Deutsche Bank and Nokia Ventures beamed $4.5 million to Thiel's Palm Pilot. "*Beep!* Money is received!" The technology worked.

But it was a misguided notion that sent Thiel and Levchin on the real path to success. As word of their creation spread, thousands of people who didn't own Palm Pilots began using the demo Web site to carry out financial transactions. What's more, eBay users began to use the demo site to transfer money online. At first, the partners found it perplexing. "I was uneasy about letting random eBay sellers and buyers use the product, especially not for its original purpose," Levchin told me. "I tried to find ways to block them. Then, we had an epiphany." The bothersome eBay users were pointing the way toward a vast and entirely unanticipated market for their creation. The two men dropped everything and focused on building a Web version of the product.

At each point, Thiel and Levchin analyzed the dynamics, made a decision, and acted swiftly. In 1999, they merged Confinity with Elon Musk's online banking firm, X.com, and named the new entity PayPal. They built a tight-knit team of zealous innovators and thoroughly revamped their business six times before selling it to eBay for $1.5 billion in 2002.

Even more remarkable is what happened next. The three founders and other members of their team, who came to be known in Silicon Valley as the PayPal mafia, went on to create a wave of innovative enterprises, including YouTube, Yelp, LinkedIn, Tesla Motors, SpaceX, SolarCity, Palantir Technologies, Founders Fund, Slide, HVF, Yammer, Geni, and Digg. And each time, they succeeded by flying the OODA loop faster and more deftly than their competitors.

Let's use the PayPal mafia to explore how creators fly the OODA loop.

THE OODA LOOP DEFINED

Years before technology innovators focused on fast-cycle iteration, lean startup methodology, or design thinking, John Boyd, an Air Force fighter pilot who served in the Korean War, crafted a framework for making rapid decisions that would ensure success in fast-changing environments. Boyd's "OODA loop"—observe, orient, decide, and act—is as pertinent to business as it is to aerial combat.

Boyd observed that even though U.S. Sabrejets climbed and

turned more slowly than opposing Soviet MiG jets, U.S. pilots almost always won dogfights. Experts credited this to the superior training of the Americans. Boyd believed it was something more.

When comparing the capabilities of the two planes, Boyd noticed that while MiGs could reach greater speeds and fly at higher altitudes, they were slower to shift between those two areas of strength. The American planes made transitions more swiftly. The ability to perform more maneuvers in less time kept U.S. pilots one step ahead. As a dogfight progressed, the enemy made decisions based on circumstances that had already changed. Repeated over and over during aerial battles, that process almost always resulted in fateful decisions that left the MiGs in flames.

"The adversary that can move through these cycles faster gains an inestimable advantage by disrupting his enemy's ability to respond effectively," Boyd testified before the Armed Services Committee of the U.S. House of Representatives.

Boyd, cocky even by fighter pilot standards, theorized that by responding decisively to rapidly changing conditions, a pilot could change the dynamics of a fight before the enemy could react, thereby confusing him and controlling the situation. At Nellis Air Force Base in Nevada, "40-Second Boyd," as he was called, challenged any pilot to defeat him in a mock dogfight, vowing that he would win in 40 seconds or pay $40. By all accounts, he never lost—even if he gave his opponent an advantage at the start.

Working with civilian mathematician Thomas Christie, Boyd developed the Energy-Maneuverability theory of aerial combat, which became the standard for fighter aircraft. He applied his mathematical skill and experience in the air to help design the F-16, a supersonic aircraft capable of extreme maneuvers. The F-16 weighs about half as much as its predecessor, the F-15, and can handily execute an advantageous high-G barrel roll, twisting and turning, even at low speeds.

Perhaps Boyd's greatest contribution is his paradigm for how to create competitive advantage in fast-paced environments. He spent years studying military history, science, mathematics, and psychology to devise a framework he called the OODA loop.

The OODA loop consists of four steps. *Observe* what is happening and process as much information from as many sources as possible. *Orient* those observations by distinguishing the relevant from the insignificant. *Decide* on a course of action and select one path. *Act* to execute the decision—keeping in mind that the action is not an end, because the loop flows continuously.

The OODA loop is not just about moving faster. It is about being able to generate the necessary time to examine a problem before taking action. By, in Boyd's words, *"getting inside the opponent's OODA Loop,"* one can operate at a faster tempo and short-circuit his process. The ability to observe, orient, decide, and act in a tighter loop obscures one's own intentions while the opponent reveals his next move. The advantage gained by reacting swiftly compounds over time, and in short order the challenger can overcome a more powerful opponent.

In today's world of instant communication, accelerated technology, and economic turbulence, success requires adapting to a constantly changing context. Creators decode the environment, take definitive action, and prevail by making adjustments swiftly. Here is how to put the OODA loop into action to outmaneuver the competition time and again.

OBSERVE

A pilot requires situational awareness—the ability to pay close attention to events as they unfold. Boyd taught pilots to identify inconsistencies between their frame of reference and the evolving reality. Those mismatches provide the opportunity to seize the advantage.

This applies to any fast-moving situation. Creators gather as much information as possible as quickly as possible. They pay attention to details and stay alert to anomalies.

"It's important to focus on the concrete particulars that are present right now," PayPal cofounder Peter Thiel explained. "People are always trying to think about how they're going to change the world, but in an increasingly globalized marketplace, it has gotten a lot more complicated to map out where something is going just by looking at where it starts."

ORIENT

Information is worthless without interpretation. Orientation involves synthesizing information to gain a cohesive understanding. It requires analyzing all stimuli and differentiating between the relevant and the meaningless to get greater insight into what a scenario might mean. Experience, traditions, industry norms, and new information contribute to accurate assessment of a dynamic situation.

To explain the orientation concept, Boyd used the analogy of building snowmobiles. He challenged people to consider four seemingly unrelated mechanical systems: a set of skis, a boat with an outboard motor, a bicycle, and a military tank. Imagine taking each apart, then combining selected parts to form a new entity. The skis supply the runners, the boat the motor, the bike the handlebars, the tank the treads. Voilà: a snowmobile. The snowmobile became Boyd's analogy for the ability to assimilate information and come up with a more sophisticated view. "A winner is someone who can build snowmobiles and employ them in appropriate fashion when facing uncertainty and unpredictable change," he said.

"One rule of thumb," Thiel told me, "is to take over a fairly narrow market with a technology that is ten times better than the next best thing. PayPal was valuable to eBay sellers because the next best alternative was a cashier's check that would arrive in seven to ten days."

"I look for distribution arbitrage," David Sacks, PayPal's first COO, said, referring to the window in which a unique distribution technique can yield a significant advantage. As with any slight edge, unusual distribution channels provide opportunities that are just as important as product features.

DECIDE

In combat, pilots must adjust for varying conditions by making quick decisions. The same decisiveness is required in business. Creators cut through ambiguity by making rapid determinations.

ACT

John Boyd taught that a winner destroys his rival's perspective on the situation by initiating a series of unexpected actions. Faced with such a twist, an opponent will often interpret the situation from a familiar standpoint. Boyd instructed pilots to take another action before the rival could switch tactics, further disorienting his frame of reference. Creators similarly take action to move nimbly and gain control of market advantages ahead of less agile competitors.

Once an action is taken, the loop begins again. As the arena shifts, our viewpoint changes. The faster we identify the difference between reality and our perception of it, the sooner we can adjust our orientation, then make a decision and implement it by taking action. Creators master fast-cycle iteration by continuously flying the OODA loop.

"One of the things that the PayPal crew was very good at doing was moving," Reid Hoffman told me. "They got it done, got it out, dropped things that weren't working, and figured it out. For example, we dropped the Palm thing about a year into it because there was no traction. We decided to focus entirely on the e-mail stuff." Hoffman, best known as cofounder of the career networking site LinkedIn, joined PayPal as vice president for business development in 1999.

The PayPal team moved quickly to observe, orient, decide, and act more effectively than larger, better-financed competitors, as well as cyberthieves who tried to steal from the site.

"Competitors made progress on certain features, but never twice," David Sacks said. "We would just see what they did and iterate." When Dotbank.com awarded $10 bonuses to those who signed friends up for a similar service, PayPal rolled out the same feature within a week: PayPal offered $10 to sign up and $10 to refer a friend. Free money is a powerful incentive.

PayPal became one of the first viral online products. "Two or three months after we launched the Palm technology, we realized e-mail was going to be a more powerful driver," Thiel told me. E-mail provided an easy way to spread the word about the payment site. When a PayPal user e-mailed money to someone without an account, that person would receive a message asking her to click a link and sign up for the service to receive payment. PayPal users could send money to anyone, whether in the system or not, as long as the recipient had an e-mail account. For a while, PayPal signed up more than 20,000 users every day.

The ability to stay ahead of the competition is at the core of the OODA loop. PayPal capitalized on this vis-à-vis eBay. At the time, eBay buyers and sellers were completing transactions by mailing checks or cash. By inviting their buyers to use PayPal, sellers would get an extra $10 on each transaction—and for sellers, margins were important. That created explosive growth for PayPal and a competitive dynamic to keep eBay off balance.

When confronted with another opportunity—a customer asked to use the PayPal logo on his auction site—PayPal quickly entered the loop again. Going one step further, it designed an "I accept PayPal" logo for eBay sellers to post. PayPal first supplied the HTML code so that users could post the logo themselves, but then realized that to make it even easier, PayPal could post the logos for them. By acting promptly, PayPal outmaneuvered the large auction site at every turn.

"eBay viewed PayPal as a parasite," Sacks said. PayPal, in effect, ran the cash registers for the online store. Meg Whitman, then CEO of eBay, counterattacked by buying Billpoint, a competing online transaction vehicle. But PayPal had a tighter loop; rapid assessment and adaptation in its ever-changing world propelled the company forward. The creator who can observe, orient, decide, and act faster prevails because the opponent is reacting to situations that have already changed.

One component of the OODA loop is making your intentions unpredictable while simultaneously reading competitors' intentions. PayPal did this when eBay's Billpoint entered into a partnership with Visa. PayPal acted quickly to offer customers a debit card with cash-back rewards. Visa threatened a lawsuit. That is when Reid Hoffman flew the OODA loop.

"The rule of thumb was that if it left the building, it was in my grip," said Hoffman, known as the firefighter-in-chief at PayPal. His responsibilities, which comprised payment infrastructure, banking relationships, regulatory conflicts, and media relations, also included dealing with Visa. Although Hoffman could not persuade the credit card giant to drop the lawsuit, he did manage to buy PayPal much-needed time by prevailing on Visa to study the market before taking action. Visa agreed to analyze the situation over the next year. That time gave PayPal the opportunity to adjust, act, and act again. PayPal's OODA loop was much tighter.

Hoffman observed that short time frames often force entrepreneurs to make decisions with minimal information. But the high speed of global competition requires a would-be creator to hone the ability to decide quickly and move.

When Thiel and Levchin's company, Confinity, merged with Elon Musk's online banking firm, X.com, selection of a CEO had to happen quickly. Skirmishes ensued. Thiel was out. Musk was in. Then Musk was out, and Thiel returned. But there wasn't time for pitched battles.

In the summer of 2000, PayPal burned through $10 million a month. Thiel had raised $100 million in capital before the tech bubble burst, but PayPal's business model proved to be flawed. "It was like a 747 pointed to the ground," Sacks said. PayPal thought it would make money on the balance that users kept in their accounts, but the users withdrew the cash. In addition, PayPal had to remit a 3 percent fee on all credit-card transactions. "There is nothing that focuses the mind like impending doom," Hoffman said.

PayPal's creators rapidly analyzed the problem and devised a new feature. To use PayPal, customers had to click an "accept" or "deny" button and agree that once their transactions reached a threshold of $1,000, subsequent receipts would be subject to a fee.

The new feature, targeted at businesses that made large-sum transactions, provided PayPal with the revenue to stay afloat.

With money flowing in, PayPal next faced organized crime rings that were siphoning funds with stolen credit card numbers. Levchin recognized the first fraudulent charge-back and monitored subsequent charge-backs intensively. At first, the loss rate was less than 1 percent. However, given the rate of growth, Levchin took immediate action. He attacked the problem before competitors grasped its magnitude.

"I noticed that it was escalating with incredible pace, not like one today, five tomorrow; it was one charge-back today and then 5,500 next week," Levchin said. "It just exploded, and within a few months we were bleeding cash out."

Levchin worked around the clock coding statistical packages to thwart cyberthieves who built automated programs that compromised thousands of accounts, transferring money between those accounts in ways that were impossible to trace. Every time PayPal tried a new fraud-prevention tactic, thieves found a way around it. Finally, Levchin devised a two-pronged solution.

Flying the OODA loop with lightning speed, he asked, "What can people do that computers can't?" His first antifraud measure used obscured letters that humans could read but computers couldn't. If the letters were not deciphered and typed in, the site couldn't be accessed. It was dubbed the "Are you a human?" test. Today, these wavy, distorted letters have become the standard by which millions of online transactions are completed.

Step two involved a complex software system Levchin named IGOR, designed to display reams of information in order to expose large movements of money. Analysts could track both financial and security risks using the technology. "We learned that there are certain problems that neither humans nor computers alone can solve," Thiel told me. "So we put processing power together with human analysts trained to spot anomalies." With the new system, PayPal saw fraud decrease significantly. Here again, the PayPal team observed, oriented, decided, and acted to stay one step ahead of fraudsters trying to pilfer money from the site.

Competitors simply quit when fraud ran rampant, but PayPal was experienced in dealing swiftly with problems. "When you can call on resources and you have a fast product iteration cycle, you have to be able to adjust quickly," Hoffman said.

PayPal turned its first profit in the first quarter of 2001, even as the tech bubble burst. Companies across Silicon Valley were closing their doors, yet in February 2002 PayPal successfully launched its IPO. In July of that year, eBay dropped Billpoint and bought PayPal for $1.5 billion.

HAVE A WINGMAN: BUILD FIERCE TEAMS

"Startups are not driven by just one person," Thiel told me. "It's a team effort and you have a lot of ups and downs, so how people stick through it matters. Prehistory matters. You don't want to start a business with someone you just met a week ago—it's like getting married to the person next to you at the slot machines in Vegas. You might hit a jackpot, but chances are pretty good that's a really bad idea."

To observe, orient, decide, and act, creators work with trusted collaborators. Thiel and Levchin built a close-knit team at PayPal, recruiting largely through networks of friends from their alma maters. Thiel, a Stanford-trained lawyer and macroeconomist, had been ranked among the top twenty chess players in the United States as an adolescent. He recruited friends from Stanford, many from *The*

Stanford Review, a libertarian magazine he had cofounded. Levchin, a native of Ukraine who narrowly escaped the 1986 Chernobyl meltdown and shortly thereafter emigrated to the United States, where he became a computer scientist, hired engineers largely from his school, the University of Illinois at Urbana-Champaign, which boasts a powerhouse computer science program.

Reid Hoffman, the first person appointed to PayPal's board of directors, was Thiel's college friend. Hoffman recounted Thiel's words: "You've been telling me, month by month, about all of your lessons as CEO of SocialNet. Why not help us?" Hoffman's first assignment as a board member came with a specific arrangement: Thiel could call at any time, and Hoffman would call back before midnight. They also went for a walk every Saturday morning to discuss what makes a startup work. Hoffman later joined the team full-time.

"I think in a big way that the reason for PayPal's success is that we had a team of really tight people who were good at different things," Levchin told me. "We pulled together, kept hammering away, and believed we could win."

To fly the OODA loop effectively, you need wingmen. In a dogfight, pilots rely not just on their individual skills but on the loyalty, skill, and commitment of their squadron. In combat, commitment to one another and to completion of the mission is essential. Military aviators practice flying in formation so that the team can perform seamlessly together. One pilot is designated as the leader. The wingmen follow the leader's movement through complicated twists and maneuvers. Their primary function is to protect the leader's blind spot, the position 180 degrees from the pilot's sight line. As roles and responsibilities change, leaders temporarily become wingmen and vice versa. They move as one.

The same applies to creators building startups. "The single biggest predictor of attrition—lethal for small companies—is how many friends employees have at work," Thiel told me. "If we want to use models, you could think of a cult being better than a factory."

Creators build loyal teams consisting of people with fiercely independent points of view. They foster the open exchange of ideas across functions and departments and cultivate vigorous debate. Building enterprises requires intellectual engagement and commitment.

At PayPal, all customer logs, revenue information, and fraud losses were discussed openly. All levels were charged with sharpening the company's goals. "At PayPal, it was definitely considered extremely inappropriate to say nothing if you thought something was wrong," Levchin said. "It didn't matter if it was to your boss or if you were the boss."

When done respectfully, sparring among teammates spurs progress. Creators ask, "What would you do differently? How can we reevaluate? What is the flaw in our assumption?" Healthy debate improves decision making and prevents the kinds of easy answers embraced by competitors.

"PayPal thrived as a group of intellectuals," said Joe Lonsdale, an intern at PayPal who went on to be a cofounder of Palantir Technologies. "You had to justify things, and there was a lot of debating back and forth and lots of focusing on a very high-level idea of what you're doing and why it's valuable." Top executives often disagreed about the best course of action. People felt free to speak up when they saw something that wasn't working and could be improved.

"I was a brash twenty-two-year-old, and I remember firing off this e-mail that disagreed with the entire executive staff," said Yelp cofounder Jeremy Stoppelman of his early days at PayPal. "I didn't get in trouble—the culture actually encouraged me to feel comfortable questioning management." Flying the OODA loop requires surrounding yourself with people unafraid to offer educated opinions about how to improve the next cycle. The PayPal creators had strong views, and stood behind them.

Too much consensus is a recipe for disaster, according to Sacks: "There is something artificial when everyone is agreeing with each other. It's useful to indulge people who don't agree, and see their viewpoint or force yourself to explain things better." Expression of diverse opinions can accelerate progress.

The healthy exchange of ideas within PayPal not only led to the creation of a successful online money-transfer Web site, but also seeded a new wave of successful startups. The PayPal mafia is widely credited with spearheading Web 2.0, the interactive consumer Internet, following the dot-com crash of 2000.

The inspiration for Yelp, for example, came over a lunch in Palo Alto in 2004. A little more than a dozen people, mostly ex-PayPal staffers, were celebrating Max Levchin's birthday. Jeremy Stoppelman and Russell Simmons, both former PayPal engineers, began musing about a system in which people could e-mail friends with recommendations for doctors, dentists, or dry cleaners.

Walking back from lunch, Stoppelman and Simmons decided to pitch the idea to Levchin as a new business concept. The next day, Levchin agreed to back the project with $1 million and provide office space. As the idea blossomed, Reid Hoffman and Peter Thiel offered guidance. When the time came to seek venture funding, Roelof Botha, PayPal's former CFO, who had become a partner at Sequoia Capital, made introductions.

Stoppelman and Simmons flew the OODA loop through multiple turns before their idea took off. Their original e-mail system focused on asking friends for recommendations and posting answers on a communal site. It failed to fly. The Yelp founders quickly observed that people seeking referrals didn't always get answers, and those being asked for recommendations became irritated by a barrage of questions.

Buried deep in the original site was a small feature called Write a Review, where anyone could offer an unsolicited opinion. It had been added as an afterthought. "Russ asked me, 'Should we have a way people can write a review without being asked a question?'" Stoppelman recalled. "I felt strongly that no one would write a review for fun, but said, 'Sure, Russ, tuck it in there.'" Even though the feature was difficult to find, early users wrote reviews. "They wrote five or ten or fifteen reviews in one sitting. People got addicted to it," Stoppelman said. "There was something interesting about review writing that we had just missed."

The Yelp founders relaunched the site four months later, in February 2005, to allow anyone to share unsolicited reviews. "We were familiar with the history of tweaks and turns that PayPal took before it really became PayPal," Stoppelman said. "That made us aware that we probably wouldn't get it right at first, and there would be this other dramatic shift. People writing a lot of reviews was the signal that allowed us to reorient and get on the right track." The Yelp founders hadn't thought anyone would enjoy writing a review of a local dry-cleaning business, but they acted quickly when they found that people actually did.

"You just have to be vigilant and open-minded to look out for those moments," Stoppelman said. In early 2008, Yelp built early applications for the iPhone that catapulted the company forward. An intern designed a prototype of what became the first augmented reality feature in the app store. The Yelp founders agreed to embed an Easter egg feature—a functionality that is hidden inside an application just for fun. Subsequently, they observed that the "geeky feature," which could overlay information about businesses by using the phone's video camera, was taking off. It allowed users to display Yelp business reviews in real time on the viewing screen of an iPhone by slowly panning the device around while walking down a street. They acted quickly to build Yelp Monocle, which increased downloads by 30 to 40 percent. Drawing on their ability to observe, orient, decide, and act quickly, the Yelp founders have built a company valued at more than $4 billion.

The founders of YouTube flew the OODA loop to capitalize on an opportunity as well. The platform that eventually became the hotspot for online video originated as a video-dating site inspired by the photo-rating forum HOTorNOT.com.

Unlike most Web sites in 2003, which were run by an administrator who approved or deleted content, HOTorNOT.com functioned as a site where anyone could upload photos that others could view. It was the first time that people who didn't own the site could provide the content. Users voluntarily submitted photos, and others rated them on a scale of 1 to 10 for attractiveness. This user-generated content fascinated Chad Hurley, Steve Chen, and Jawed Karim.

As they moved to design a site able to support user-generated dating videos, they observed that their beta-site audience was intensely interested in a video of Karim at the San Diego Zoo. In a nineteen-second clip called "Me at the Zoo," Karim stands before the elephant enclosure and says, "The cool thing about these guys is that they have really, really, really long trunks, and that's cool. And that's pretty much all there is to say." Why did people care about Karim's zoo visit? It wasn't clear, but the creators of what would soon become YouTube noticed a mismatch between this new information and their original intention. For the online world, it seemed, nondating activities were as compelling as video classifieds—perhaps even more.

These creators decided that a dating site was too limited. They considered the idea of helping people share videos for online auctions. Then they opened their site for general use. Within months, people began posting videos of pets, practical jokes, classroom lectures, and travel adventures. From their days as PayPal engineers, the YouTube founders understood the importance of growing through an existing distribution platform. Hurley, Chen, and Karim made HTML code available for people to embed in their profiles from MySpace, the dominant social network at the time. YouTube's growth piggybacked on MySpace until the founders sold the site to Google for $1.65 billion in 2006.

"With the consumer Internet, if you're not embarrassed by your first product release, you've launched too late," Reid Hoffman told me. "Everyone wants their product to be shiny, great, and revolutionary, so they take too long in the development cycle to build this really shiny thing, when in fact time really matters."

An OODA loop veteran, Hoffman observed that people were using avatars and screen names to disguise their personal identities for social purposes. He saw a need to build a professional online network and in 2002 began developing a business application for social media that would go beyond dating, entertainment, or photo sharing—and he executed quickly and decisively.

On May 5, 2003, LinkedIn went live. But growth was glacial. As few as twenty people joined per day. At PayPal, Hoffman had experienced viral growth. He designed LinkedIn to expand similarly through invitations sent from one professional to another. Yet he noticed that people wanted to know who else was using LinkedIn so that they could decide whether to join: "Is this an empty club or a network with people?" Hoffman put it.

When he added the AddressBook feature to let users see which of their contacts were already using LinkedIn, the site gained traction. Creators have to observe (notice what customers are doing), orient (interpret that information), decide (determine a course of action), and act (change the site's features). Hoffman described the process as "flexible persistence." By 2014, LinkedIn had connected more than 332 million members and exceeded $2 billion in revenue. The company is valued at $27 billion.

Following PayPal's sale to eBay, Peter Thiel launched the global macro hedge fund Clarium Capital and started a venture capital fund, Founders Fund. He also considered new business opportunities with Joe Lonsdale, Stephen Cohen, Alex Karp, and Nathan Gettings, and in 2004, he pursued the idea of creating an enterprise software tool similar to PayPal's IGOR to thwart terrorists. Palantir Technologies resulted. Today, Palantir—which takes its name from the "seeing stones" in *The Lord of the Rings*—designs powerful enterprise software that can scan multiple data sources at once.

"At PayPal, we started with one idea and kept changing it, found something that worked, and went with it," said Lonsdale, who had been a software engineer at PayPal. "It's the same at Palantir. If you have the flexibility to iterate quickly, it lets design evolve over time."

Using Palantir's information-sifting tool, intelligence analysts can spot patterns such as suspicious registrations for flight schools. For instance, prior to the 9/11 attacks, five of the nineteen hijackers used the same phone number as ringleader Mohamed Atta to book their airline tickets. Today, with Palantir, such obscure connections would be much more likely to come to light.

The technology company has helped track down Osama bin Laden, thwart roadside bombings in Iraq, unmask suicide-bombing networks in Afghanistan, and identify drug cartels in Mexico. This unlikely Silicon Valley startup gives the CIA, the U.S. Defense Department, and the FBI data-mining tools to extract information and act on it.

The Palantir founders had to observe, orient, decide, and act to overcome problems hidden below the surface that no one in Palo Alto had anticipated. "In Silicon Valley, we were accustomed to a clean system of structured data," Lonsdale said. The government agencies responsible for national security, on the other hand, must sort through massive amounts of unstructured data and sparse data, "some of which you can trust and some of which you can't." Other concerns—such as who can access the information, how to track who had seen it, how to protect it from external threats—compounded government data problems. Palantir had to restructure its technology to create a solution.

"When you find out that there is an iceberg that is going to destroy your ship, you don't go around saying, 'The business model forces us to go in this direction.' You say, 'There is an iceberg there. We've got to blow that thing up, or go around it, or we've got to create an antigravity machine,'" Palantir CEO Alex Karp told a recent Palantir Government Conference. "Whatever we have to do, we're going to do it."

Flying the OODA loop, the Palantir team worked nonstop to build Raptor, a more powerful program able to index structured and unstructured data on a huge scale from both trusted and untrusted sources. For nearly three years, Palantir engineers worked side-by-side with intelligence analysts to revise the search tool through iterative collaboration to enable analysts to interact with the data and make intelligent connections. In 2014, Palantir Technologies reached nearly $1 billion in revenue. The company is valued at $9 billion.

"There are just tons of problems in the world that are currently being solved through pattern recognition when we have the data to do more precise analysis and come up with better solutions," Max Levchin told me. He was explaining why he has flown the OODA loop yet again starting HVF—Hard Valuable Fun.

HVF explores and funds efforts to use data to solve significant human problems and create new market efficiencies. In 2004 Levchin founded Slide, a media-sharing service that he sold to Google in 2010 for $182 million. He also helped start Yelp and serves as chairman of its board. But HVF, founded in 2011, brought Levchin back to his passion: "geeking out on data."

"There's a great parallel to PayPal. The financial industry had rules for fraud created without analyzing thousands of variables," Levchin explained. "But PayPal had millions of observations because we lost so much money and that meant we could build IGOR, a precise model to thwart the bad guys. We used data in a crusade against evildoers."

With HVF, Levchin observed an explosion of data collected through low-cost sensors and decided to exploit it by applying his technical and business skills in fields hobbled by "painfully inefficient" processes. Two companies had spun out of HVF by mid-2014: Glow and Affirm.

Observing the broken health-care system in the United States, Levchin oriented to attack the problem from a fresh perspective. Instead of focusing directly on rising costs, he zeroed in on making it cheaper to stay healthy.

"Humans are good at behaving badly and not very good at changing their habits," Levchin told me. " 'I'll start that diet tomorrow. Tonight, I'll have cheesecake.' That's pretty normal." But what if people were given actionable health data that showed them the results of their behavior?

Levchin focused on heart disease. He built a prototype of a device that would detect water retention around the heart and sound an alert if the user needed immediate care. But health insurance providers expressed little interest.

Quickly reorienting, Levchin decided to become the "white knight" of one of the dozens of medical conditions that are largely neglected by big players in the field. In 2013 he launched Glow, an app for women trying to get pregnant. He targeted infertility because treatment is rarely covered by health insurance, even though the problem is becoming more common as a result of the trend toward having children later in life. Using data and machine learning, the Glow app combines a calendar with data inputs from women such as menstrual cycle, basal body temperature, emotional state, and vitamin intake to reveal a woman's days of optimal fertility.

Glow also adds a novel twist on health insurance. Couples who use the app can opt to contribute $50 a month to a pooled fund. After 10 months, the fund is split equally among those who haven't been successful, to help them pay for fertility treatments.

"Once we have a few hundred thousand data points, we'll know a lot more about infertility," Levchin said. With all that data in hand, he'll once again observe, orient, decide, and act to press the attack on infertility.

Since 2012, Levchin has also flown the OODA loop as founder and CEO of Affirm, an innovative consumer-lending company. "Credit information used today to apply for a home loan, or car loan, or credit card is low-quality and primitive," Levchin said. Today's widely used FICO scores are a product of the 1970s, when only a few kinds of data on consumers' behavior were available. Affirm uses tens of thousands of data points to assess a person's creditworthiness, drawing on everything from social media profiles to mobile phone data. Affirm evaluates consumers' credit with a process that Levchin says is better than traditional risk calculations.

Qualified borrowers can make purchases online with what

Levchin described as a "digital tab" that they can pay off later. Loans extend up to $10,000 for consumers. For merchants, Affirm provides a risk-free way to approve purchases on credit with loans guaranteed by Levchin's startup.

"We'll see if we can take down the too-big-to-fail guys," Levchin told me. Given his proven ability to observe, orient, decide, and act quickly, they have reason to be worried.

David Sacks, PayPal's first COO, may be the company's most proficient OODA loop flier. Sacks is credited with devising PayPal's "accept" or "deny" product feature that charged businesses the cost of transactions at a crucial moment in PayPal's early history.

After PayPal was sold, Sacks moved to Hollywood, started Room 9 Entertainment, and produced the movie *Thank You for Smoking*. In 2006, he cofounded Geni.com, a genealogy Web site conceived as a family social network for sharing information among relatives.

"But by 2007, it became pretty clear to me that Facebook was going to eat the family social-networking space," Sacks said. He observed the Facebook threat, decided to focus Geni.com more narrowly on genealogy, and acted to reposition his social networking team to work on corporate applications, a move that would lead to Yammer, a social network that has a user interface similar to Facebook's but customized for corporate purposes.

In developing Yammer, Sacks identified a market need inside large corporations to communicate better and to more effectively coordinate work flow on projects across fragmented units. "We solve a lot of Dilbert problems," Sacks said. "These are questions like, Who are my coworkers? What are they working on? How can I contribute? What is going on across other projects and teams?"

Sacks sought a product "hook," a simple behavior people would engage in daily, like the exchange of money at PayPal. In combination with a work chart detailing in-process projects, conversations around the question "What are you working on?" sparked viral growth at Yammer. The company provides alerts, notifications, private messages, and news feeds from different project teams and coworkers. Colleagues post communications, files, presentations, links, questions, videos, polls, or other work-related content.

"I would never start a company if I merely had a good product idea," Sacks told me. "You have to have a good distribution idea as well."

Sacks designed a "freemium" distribution strategy, unveiling Yammer as a free site anyone in a company could start using without waiting for software or permission. An employee can sign up and invite coworkers to join. As more employees use Yammer, corporations view the system as a valuable resource and pay to upgrade the service, add features, and obtain administrative control.

Of course, Sacks's own "law of distribution arbitrage" told him that the window of opportunity he had opened would all too quickly let in copycats who would replicate Yammer's growth strategy. OODA loop fliers understand that they must continue to evolve.

Sacks emphasizes the need to "go from lean to mean" before imitators follow. Within a year after launching Yammer, he had raised $140 million and employed 200 people. "I believe in the lean startup model only until it clicks," he said. "If we were in lean mode and had a small team of fifteen to twenty employees when Salesforce launched Chatter, we'd probably be crushed like a bug." Sacks sold Yammer to Microsoft in 2012 for $1.2 billion.

THE ENDLESS OODA LOOP

What is the secret of the PayPal mafia? How is it that these creators can start and scale companies so successfully time and again?

"PayPal was quite an extreme learning experience," Peter Thiel said. "The high-level lesson that people learned was that things are hard, but if you really work at it, you can get it to work." Thiel explained that in a lot of other contexts, things either work automatically or don't work at all. "If someone spent their whole life at Microsoft, it would be pretty straightforward," he said. "On the other hand, if you had been at a company that failed, it would be unclear what the correct lesson would be." The PayPal experience was "right in between" and taught a valuable set of lessons.

All of PayPal's early team members were young, competitive, curious, and ready to move through multiple iterations to make something work. Two companies, Confinity and X.com, combined pools of talented people, and acquisition by eBay freed up that talent and provided them with capital early in their careers. The PayPal mafia saw how a successful company was built and went out to do it again. As their careers progressed, they supported each other's next endeavors.

Flying the OODA loop becomes instinctive with practice. Regardless of the battlefield, anyone—not just the PayPal mafia—can fly it. Each of us can learn to observe, orient, decide, and act to stay one step ahead.

Chapter 4

FAIL WISELY

Ever tried. Ever failed. No matter. Try again. Fail again.
Fail better.

—Samuel Beckett

Creators share one trait: failure.

Some fail early. Most fail often. Almost all of them will fail again. But something deeper occurs as a result: Failure provokes learning.

As we hatch new ideas, we discover that much of what we would like to predict is unpredictable. Creators inevitably miss the mark. Difficult conversations, surprising outcomes, and product flaws occur constantly. It's neither fun nor comfortable, but failure is necessary.

"I learned a whole bunch of lessons from the failure at Social-

Net," Reid Hoffman said, referring to his first company, a site that connected people based on common interests. "Given our culture of prototyping, we have had tons of failed prototypes when we are creating products and services," said David Kelley, cofounder of design firm IDEO. "One of the things that's great about Silicon Valley is that failure is a badge of honor because people here value the learning that goes on."

Creators cultivate an ability to be truly—sometimes brutally—honest with themselves about success and failure; at the same time, they maintain a resolve that helps them learn from mistakes. "You have to ask friends to tell you what they see," Elon Musk said. "They don't want to hurt your feelings, but they can see where you're going wrong, often before you can." Creators are transparent about shortcomings and acknowledge when they need help. Self-awareness is crucial. They don't hide from failure or hide failure from others.

In fact, creators welcome small failures as a way to push themselves. "What have you failed at today?" That's the question Sara Blakely's father asked each night at the dinner table. She failed at sports. She failed at singing. She failed to achieve a good score on the LSAT several times, and she had doors slammed in her face when she worked as a fax machine sales rep. But failure didn't stop her when she tried to patent an innovative undergarment. And failure didn't stop her from founding Spanx and becoming America's youngest self-made female billionaire.

Even the world's greatest talents rarely succeed on their first attempt. Ernest Hemingway rewrote the ending to *A Farewell to Arms* thirty-nine times before publishing his manuscript. Alfred Hitchcock shot the shower scene in *Psycho* seventy-eight times to get the harrowing moment exactly right. Vincent van Gogh described his creative process as "repetitions," painting and repainting versions of a single composition. Ludwig van Beethoven composed symphonies by making hundreds of deletions, corrections, and deep pockmarks in the pages.

Why would creating a company be any less difficult? Why wouldn't it be *more* difficult? Business creators work on a canvas of market fluctuations. Whereas traditional business leaders often pursue efficiency to minimize risk, creators of new enterprises learn from mistakes about how to proceed.

"When nothing was working, venture capital firm Y Combinator cofounder Paul Graham gave us permission to get out of our comfort zone and go talk to people using our service in New York," Airbnb cofounder Joe Gebbia said. Deciding to get up close and personal with their failures, Gebbia and Brian Chesky booked listings with Airbnb hosts, stayed in their homes, and talked with them over the breakfast table. One simple thing they learned was that would-be renters often posted photos that didn't show their apartments in the best light. So the budding creators rented cameras and shot photos to showcase the available lodgings.

Theranos founder Elizabeth Holmes said, "Our premise starting out was that we might have to fail a thousand times, but we would get it to work. We joked about calling our product 'The Edison,'" referring to Thomas Edison's famous quote, "I have not failed, I've just found 10,000 ways that won't work."

Creators become comfortable with being uncomfortable. To fail wisely, they place small bets, set a failure ratio, believe enough to persist, and turn setbacks into strength. Let's delve into just how they develop the skill to fail wisely.

PLACE SMALL BETS

"You have to see failure as the beginning and the middle, but never entertain it as an end," said Jessica Herrin, founder of Stella & Dot.

"A lot of times people ask me, 'When did you know it would work?' Always! I always knew. I just never expected it to be one of the first ten things I tried."

In 2003, Herrin rearranged beads on the crafts table in the sunroom of her home in Austin, Texas. She stared at the bright baubles and spools of wire, determined to figure out how to turn them into a viable business. Her house had filled up with do-it-yourself jewelry kits, educational games, customized greeting cards, and other direct-selling ideas. Three months pregnant, she had a deadline.

An e-commerce manager for Dell Computer, Herrin had followed her husband to Texas for his career. Despite her success in corporate America, she wanted to "solve the modern woman's dilemma," as she put it. What women needed, Herrin felt, was independent, flexible work. She set out to devise a solution.

Quite unexpectedly, the idea hit her during an off moment in a Dallas hotel. As she rode an elevator filled with cosmetics saleswomen attending a Mary Kay conference, Herrin felt an outpouring of energy from these independent businesswomen wearing Mary Kay sashes, tiaras, and diamond-encrusted rings, as they exchanged sales tips, proud of their accomplishments. That was it. She set out to update the model with modern social-selling tools and started a company called Luxe Jewels.

"I probably did over 100 parties and 100 trunk shows before I got to the right one with the right product," Herrin said. "I made my own jewelry. I made the invitations. And I made the Web site. I did everything."

Herrin believes in placing small bets at every turn. Taking her idea from trunk show to trunk show, she used trial and error to determine what worked and what didn't. Her original concept of handcrafted jewelry worked, but not well enough. "When I realized it wasn't all-the-way right, I had to change it," Herrin said. "I had to fail."

In 2004, Herrin and a partner, Blythe Harris, launched Stella & Dot as a "just us girls" direct-selling company that mobilizes independent consultants, called stylists, to sell fashion-forward jewelry directly to consumers online and through at-home shows. Stella & Dot, named after their grandmothers, blends person-to-person in-home sales with a mobile app, video features with styling tips, and personalized Web sites for stylists to sell the products.

"People spend way too much money making lofty mistakes," Herrin said, showing me her latest jewelry line at her headquarters in San Mateo, California. "We'll test something on a small level before we go for $1 million worth of inventory and sell it on a big level. That's an easy one."

By placing small bets, Herrin manages failure wisely. Today, she enlists Stella & Dot stylists in the trial-and-error process of selecting products. For example, she distributes colored Post-it notes at organizational meetings so that attendees can say "Love it" or "Lose it" by sticking feedback on each product display. Frontline sellers of Stella & Dot merchandise vote on necklaces, earrings, bracelets, catalog covers, and product samples in home trunk shows. By testing small sets of inventory with large numbers of stylists, Herrin front-loads failures before making big investments.

"I try to have this framework for decisions, which is, 'How do I fire bullets before cannonballs so when I recalibrate my target, I still have gunpowder enough to do the big thing?'" Herrin said. "So I'm taking calculated risks. We have got to have enough gunpowder in the business to make sure to continue our growth."

When considering expansion to the United Kingdom, Herrin heard that English women were more reserved and would not want to open their homes to sell Stella & Dot products. To test this assumption, she did seven trunk shows in five days there, visiting women in their living rooms to ask directly whether the model would work. She learned that, with a few tweaks, it would. In 2011, Stella & Dot launched internationally. Today women across the United Kingdom, Germany, France, and Ireland host Stella & Dot trunk shows in their homes.

"When you start a business, you just assume that somebody else knows the answer, if you could only figure it out," Herrin said. "Actually, nobody knows the answers 100 percent of the time. Instead, the goal is to say, 'I'm trying these three things, and one of them is going to work out.'"

With more than $220 million in sales in 2013, Stella & Dot continues to grow. And more than 16,000 stylists—from a soccer mom in Dallas and a college student in Manhattan to a grandmother in Miami and a physician in San Francisco—place their own small bets by hosting Stella & Dot trunk shows for friends.

"Our goal isn't to make the most money this year," Herrin said. "What I tell my board is that it is to experiment and learn so that we can be a bigger and better company next year and the year beyond. I want Stella & Dot to be a great company for generations to come, and that takes a lot of failure and willingness to nurture that in your organization."

THE MARSHMALLOW CHALLENGE

Peter Skillman, an executive at Nokia, launched an experiment in 2002 when he was head of user experience for digital device maker Palm. It was a design competition that would come to be known as the "Marshmallow Challenge."

The experiment was straightforward. Teams of four were given eighteen minutes to build the tallest freestanding structure possible using twenty strands of spaghetti, a meter of tape, a marshmallow, and a piece of string. The marshmallow was required to be on top. How do you approach the problem?

Skillman spent five years running the design challenge with more than seven hundred people in various groups—including business school students, Taiwanese telecom engineers, University of Tokyo graduates, and managers of Fortune 500 companies. He shared his findings in a 2007 Gel conference, an annual gathering of customer experience–focused innovators.

As expected, engineers fared well. They found ways to assemble spaghetti to hold the weight of the marshmallow. Business school students were the worst. They spent too much time planning, organizing, laying out spaghetti, and debating (as Skillman described it) who would become CEO of Spaghetti, Inc.

Who were the best performers? Kindergarten students. How did kindergartners beat highly trained engineers? They didn't worry about failure. They wasted no time—they didn't sit around talking about how a marshmallow tower would look or jockeying for position or outlining a perfect strategy—they threw themselves fearlessly into the task. Kindergartners didn't think there would be one right answer. They experimented, quickly discarding what didn't work. With each try, they got feedback and tried again.

The structures the children created varied wildly but reached an average of twenty-five inches in height. Engineers with advanced degrees and years of experience found ways to support the marshmallow only at twenty-four inches of height. Kindergarteners were also the only group that asked for more spaghetti. Adults didn't question the rules, whereas children were unconstrained by convention.

"If you have a short amount of time, it's more important that you fail," Skillman said. "Fail early to succeed soon."

Unafraid of failure, kindergarteners succeeded by learning from mistakes.

PUSH THE "GO BUTTON"

In the summer of 2004, researchers from California State University put yellow hangers on the knobs of 981 front doors in a neighborhood in San Marcos, California, asking people to conserve energy. Printed on the door hangers were persuasive messages in English and Spanish with a graphic icon illustrating energy conservation suggestions: "You can save $54 dollars a month," or "You can save the planet," or "You can be a good citizen." None of these messages worked. A fourth sign read: "Seventy-seven percent of your neighbors turned off their air-conditioning and turned on their fans. Please join them." That message worked. Homeowners cut their energy use. Social pressure proved a powerful motivator—more powerful than financial incentive or moral persuasion.

The experiment inspired Dan Yates and Alex Laskey to investigate behavioral science as a means to decrease energy consumption. Similar to those door hangers, Yates and Laskey placed small bets of their own.

"Dan had a 'push-the-go-button' model that I thought was very cheesy, and still do, but it's useful," Laskey said. "We agreed to explore a lot of different paths at once to see if we could do something together that would have a positive impact on the environment. If we got to a place where we felt good enough about an idea to pursue it, then we would 'push the go button' and stop looking at the other things and really commit to it." The duo explored recycling refrigerators, upgrading appliances to improve energy efficiency, and manufacturing solar panels, among other ideas.

The potential to shift consumers' energy habits using behavioral science resonated for these college friends. Yates, a computer scientist, had founded Edusoft, an educational assessment software company. "I'd worked on a bunch of losing political campaigns," Laskey said. He also had experience working with political entities on public opinion issues, including energy efficiency.

Traveling from Arlington, Virginia, to attend a solar conference at Stanford University, Yates and Laskey arrived a few hours early and decided to cold-call City of Palo Alto Utilities to pitch their consumer behavior idea. They walked through the doors and, to their surprise, the director of marketing met with them. "If you guys do this, we'll be your first customer," he told them. Laskey decided then that they should focus on energy usage to drive efficiency gains. "Are you crazy? This is Palo Alto, not America," Yates said to his friend.

Placing another small bet, they phoned a contact in the state energy office in Texas and were invited to attend a meeting of Texas state legislators in April 2007. Yates and Laskey flew to Austin. "We shared a bedroom for four days and created a ruckus in the state legislature," Yates recalled. A Texas state congressman told them he would support their "cute idea" and write it into House Bill 3693, but if anyone objected, the consumer efficiency experiment would be killed. The bill passed. Yates and Laskey won again.

"If California hippies and Texas Republicans liked the idea, we figured we were on to something," Laskey said.

Later that year, they launched Opower, a company that delivers personalized, comparative home energy reports. Each report details the customer's energy usage plus that of 100 nearby homes of roughly the same square footage and suggests ways to improve efficiency, such as turning off electronics and lighting when not at home, insulating the attic, caulking around doors, and upgrading to energy-efficient lighting and appliances.

The Sacramento Municipal Utility District expressed interest in the idea but wanted a carbon calculator instead. "We built a carbon calculator for them in just two weeks," Yates said. "That's how we convinced them to experiment with our idea." It was another small bet.

The Sacramento utility became Opower's first client. The utility began delivering reports to some of its 1.1 million consumers. Happy faces denoted households that were energy efficient, and frowning faces denoted households that consumed more energy than their neighbors. "People didn't like it," Yates said, so the utility dropped the frowning faces. That small bet failed.

In Minnesota, Connexus Energy, another early Opower client, sent consumers a "below average" message if their energy use exceeded their neighbors'. People didn't respond well to being called below average: now consumers are told they "use more energy than neighbors."

Not all small bets pay off. Opower's effort to create an app to build social capabilities among Facebook friends failed to gain traction. "It was definitely a disappointment," Yates said. "Momentum fell away, and we ultimately decided just to walk away from it."

Overall, however, the consumer behavior experiment worked. Targeted energy reports sent to utility customers have helped lower energy usage by an average of 2 to 3 percent. Knowing what neighbors are doing changes behavior.

In 2013, Yates and Laskey experimented again: they attempted to reduce peak demand on the grid. Partnering with the Baltimore utility BGE, Opower customized text, e-mail, and phone messages to customers about how to trim electricity use during high-demand periods. Messages suggested small changes, such as adjusting the thermostat, delaying laundry, and running the dishwasher after peak hours. The experiment reduced residential consumption by 5 percent during peak times.

The company continues to lay down small bets today, and its more than ninety utility partners add up to a sizable result. "Opower's current run-rate savings are equivalent to powering all the homes in the city of Miami for a year," Laskey said, just before the company went public in April 2014. "And our cumulative savings since the company started are five terawatts, or enough energy to take all 1.3 million homes in the Granite State—New Hampshire—off the grid for a year."

"Before you realize that you're failing, you're testing," Gilt Groupe co-founder Alexandra Wilkis Wilson explained. "You can call these tests failures, but we take them as ways of learning and capturing and analyzing data. Sometimes tests perform shockingly well, and sometimes you learn from them and think, 'I could have done a better job.'"

Creators test ideas in low-risk experiments and quickly, creatively, and inexpensively gather insights to determine whether a product or idea will take off. By taking small risks, they avoid catastrophic mistakes.

"Failure is something you know only in hindsight," Handle co-founder and Menlo Ventures partner Shawn Carolan said. As an entrepreneur trying to solve e-mail overload with Handle, a software application, Carolan calls the twists and turns "pivots" that reveal failure only in retrospect. Creators try several approaches to find out what will work and what will not.

Steven Dow, a professor at Carnegie Mellon University's Human-Computer Interaction Institute, has devoted significant resources to the practice of enlightened trial and error. Making a concerted effort to experiment, reevaluate, and regroup, Dow shows that experiments yield better results than simply trying to perfect one concept, product, or idea.

To explore this principle, Dow and his colleagues conducted a simple experiment borrowed from high school physics. They gathered two groups to participate in an egg-drop competition. The object was to design a container that would keep an egg from breaking when dropped to the floor. Each group was given materials—pipe cleaners, Popsicle sticks, poster board, rubber bands, foam, tissue paper—and had twenty-five minutes to design a container and fifteen minutes to build the final design before the egg-drop test.

But there was one difference between the groups. Participants in the control group had only one egg. Each of these individuals would design, construct, and test a device using that egg. Participants in the prototyping group, however, each had a carton of eggs. They were encouraged to conduct test drops at the five, ten, fifteen, and twenty-five minute marks during the design phase. These individuals could test multiple designs.

For nearly a half-hour, each individual in the control group worked to design a single device that would protect an egg. These people were devoted to the final product and wanted it to be perfect. Participants in the prototyping group, however, created device after device, combining materials and applying an array of designs, techniques, and ideas. Instead of being focused on perfecting one design, these experimenters stress-tested their vessels, improving their parachutes, suspension systems, damping stilts, and nests for catching their egg. Multiple drops allowed them to see the outcomes.

Participants entered the build phase of the experiment with the knowledge they had gained in the design phase. Then the tests began: eggs were dropped from increasingly higher points until they broke. The devices created by those who had been allowed to break more eggs in the design phase performed better. On average, the prototyping participants' eggs were safe up to 6.1 feet; the other participants' eggs survived only up to 3.3 feet.

Despite having the same materials and time, the individuals who were allowed to learn from failure and redesign their systems performed better. They discovered the flaws and constraints and used multiple tests to inform improvements. They also learned through practice how to build the same device multiple times. Nonprototyping participants could only speculate about how their devices would perform. Placing small bets contributed to the success of those able to fail wisely.

SET A FAILURE RATIO

How much failure is acceptable? Ten percent? Twenty percent? More? In my research, I found that a surprising number of creators decide that ratio ahead of time. They aim not for perfection but to ensure that they take enough risk. Being prepared for a certain number of failures allows them to experiment to find the way forward. They take a holistic view of failure, recognizing that even blunders often have value.

Creators are thoughtful about failure in ways most of us are not. In a session with CIA analysts, In-Q-Tel founder Gilman Louie offered a pointed lesson about counterproductive attitudes toward failure. In-Q-Tel is a strategic venture fund created to foster technology companies whose products can help the U.S. intelligence community. Louie pointed out to the analysts that many of them weren't thinking clearly about the risks they were willing to take in their work. He was surprised at how courageous they could be in one kind of situation and risk averse in another.

"If terrorists rolled a hand grenade down the middle of a room," Louie said, "all of you would jump out of your seats and throw your body on it to protect everyone else. You would all give up your lives for one another and your country. However, if someone ran into the room and said, 'I need someone to make a decision, but if it's the wrong one it will be the end of your career,' all of you would run toward the door. It strikes me as odd that people at this agency will risk their lives for God and country, but not their careers."

A case officer raised her hand and offered a wry explanation. "If I jump on the hand grenade and die," she said, "I don't have to live with it afterward."

Yes, failure can be frightening. Its real cost, however, is not as great as we think.

"You have to change the way you think to say that it's okay to fail, just not catastrophically," Louie said, examining the dilemma. "To do that, don't look at the probability or success of any one item; instead, evaluate your performance in the context of a portfolio. It's a nuance, but an important distinction."

Creators don't fear failure. Instead, they find ways to soften its impact. One way is to take the focus off individual failures and evaluate results in a larger context. In the investing world, for example, even Warren Buffett can't consistently pick a bundle of stocks that are all winners. The most successful investors get ahead by choosing more winners than losers.

Most often, they worry if they experience too *few* failures. "An important metric we've talked about is making sure that we have a sufficient number of failures," eBay founder Pierre Omidyar said. "Continuing to do what you did to get where you are is a recipe for the end."

The optimal failure ratio is specific to the creator and may be higher or lower depending on the organization, industry, and culture. As a rule of thumb, the lower the cost of failure, the higher the failure ratio can potentially be. "I have it roughly in my mind, sort of one out of three times I want to fail at something," Stella & Dot founder Jessica Herrin said. "It's a sustainable balance of success." If you're not failing, Herrin believes, you're probably not being aggressive enough.

"Frankly, if you tune it so that you have zero chance of failure, you usually also have zero chance of success," LinkedIn cofounder Reid Hoffman said. "The key is to look at ways for when you get to your failure checkpoint, you know to stop." Creators set time and financial limits to know when to shift.

As companies grow successful, risk tolerance shrinks. At large companies such as eBay, failure ratios are often set too low. "When you're successful, everyone wants you to keep doing what it was that made you successful," Omidyar said. "That's everybody from your customers, to your employees, to your management, and even your board of directors. But in a fast-changing environment, you have to fight against the desire to just keep doing what worked before."

Individuals come to realize that making mistakes by pushing boundaries and testing new ideas actually might be wise.

In 2005, Eric Schmidt, then CEO of Google, outlined his 70-20-10 formula for management efforts: spend 70 percent of management's time at Google improving its core business of search and advertising; allocate 20 percent to adjacent businesses related to the core businesses such as Google Earth; and spend the remaining 10 percent exploring completely new ideas. This metric helps management prioritize innovation while focusing on existing operations. Google engineers may devote 20 percent of company time to pursuing side projects of personal interest. Some of Google's most renowned products, such as Gmail, have emerged from the engineers' experimental time. "Our goal is to have more at-bats per unit of time and effort than anyone else in the world," Schmidt said.

For venture capitalists who fund creators of new companies, failure ratios can surpass 70 percent. Of ten investments, only one or two typically produce significant returns. "What we are looking for are winners to be ten-times winners or more," Menlo Ventures partner Shawn Carolan said. "So we are looking for big markets and a dynamic that can lead an entrepreneur to grow really fast." Carolan was an early investor in Siri, the voice-command personal assistant now owned by Apple. He also backed Uber, the on-demand transportation company that connects passengers with drivers of vehicles for hire through a mobile app. "We're always looking for companies that make it so much better that you can't imagine going back," Carolan said. "When people try it, they're hooked. Those are powerful forces of nature." Carolan has had misses, too. He has turned down companies that went on to great success such as Evernote, Pandora, Trulia, and Redfin.

Companies fail for countless reasons. Sometimes ideas hatch before their time. "There was Friendster, and then there was Facebook," Patrick Chung, a partner at New Enterprise Associates, observed. Sometimes entrepreneurs are good at addressing one particular customer base but not another. Chung recently backed two entrepreneurs to start a company called Storably, an online consumer marketplace for unused space in people's basements and driveways. "We tried out a thousand different things, but it just didn't work, so we decided to wind down that business," Chung said. "But we backed the same entrepreneurs when they decided immediately to start an image analytics company called Curalate. This time, they have over 400 brands as customers, and 50 percent of the top fifty U.S. retailers. It's working unbelievably well." Sometimes internal team dynamics deteriorate. "I zoom right in on team-oriented questions," Peter Thiel said, describing how he evaluates investments at Founders Fund. "It's a lot easier to change the business model than to change the team of people."

And sometimes, technology or markets move in a different direction. "Breakout ideas seem crazy at the beginning and are often binary," Charles Hudson, partner at SoftTech VC, said. "If the world goes right or it goes left, that can create a big outcome or bury a team." The category has to be viable, and the team has to win. That may sound simple, but achieving those things simultaneously is difficult. "But if you take two entrepreneurs and put them side by side, and they're exactly identical except that one's failed massively and the other hasn't, I'd invest in the first over the latter," said Matt Cohler, general partner of Benchmark, a venture capital firm. "Learning from failure makes you a more valuable asset."

Creators believe they are never as good—or bad—as they might feel in any one moment. They experience ups and downs on a daily basis when building new enterprises. To manage this, creators measure their careers over long periods of time. This puts failure in a larger context and lessens one-time wins or losses.

Once we realize that we can fail even if we do everything "right" in a fast-changing environment, setting a failure ratio becomes a smart thing to do. Pushing our own boundaries to test our abilities helps us grow and prepare for what might come next. If we set our failure ratio too high and experience too many setbacks, it can be adjusted downward. Our own ratio may change, based not only on what industry and job we are in but also at different points in our career, depending on family, finances, health, or other concerns. The key is to set a failure ratio that is greater than zero.

BELIEVE ENOUGH TO PERSIST

"It feels like chewing glass and staring into the abyss," said Elon Musk, talking over the clanking noise of a conveyor on the Tesla factory floor. He was talking about what it's like to start a company.

For Musk, 2012 marked a turnaround. But getting there wasn't easy. Four years earlier, he had plowed all of his savings into his fledgling car company. The 2008 recession left his startup with almost no chance. But Musk dug deeper. To build an all-electric vehicle, he even borrowed money from friends.

Musk's idea was different from anything in Detroit. Traditional auto manufacturers produce high-volume, low-price hybrids. Musk inverted the approach. The Tesla Roadster would be a low-volume, high-performance sports car that would drive like a Ferrari and go from 0 to 60 in 4.4 seconds but be electric in every sense, with 7,000 tiny batteries—if he could get it on the road.

With cash running out and auto industry experts keeping a Tesla deathwatch, investors assembled for an emergency meeting. Who really thought an Internet entrepreneur could build a car, anyway?

In a boardroom of naysayers, Musk anted up his last dime. He was resolutely in. Not only that, he promised to refund customers' deposits if Tesla failed to deliver. His resolve stunned investors. Musk's commitment persuaded legendary venture capitalist Steve Jurvetson to invest alongside him. Kimbal, Elon's brother and a Tesla Motors board member, said there was no doubt that Elon would persevere even if he had no money at all. Musk closed a financing round on December 24 in the last hour of the last day before the company would go bankrupt.

"You have to be willing to go through a lot of grief, honestly. Work super hard and put a lot at risk. And it won't be comfortable," Musk said.

The trials and tribulations of Tesla Motors were painful, lengthy, and public. Engineering delays, cost overruns, and quality issues stalled production of the Roadster and more than doubled expenses. In 2007, Musk realized it was costing Tesla $140,000 per car in raw materials alone, when the sticker price of a Roadster was $92,000. He fired cofounder Martin Eberhard, Tesla's CEO, invested the last of his personal fortune, and stepped in as CEO.

Five years of designs and redesigns had failed to produce the much-anticipated Roadster. "The original thought was, we would license the chassis from the Lotus Elise and license some powertrain technology from AC Propulsion, and put those two together, and get something to market fast that just worked," Musk said. "That was wrong, and in retrospect extremely dumb."

Although the idea that Tesla could borrow off-the-shelf technology was appealing, the Roadster turned out to be 30 percent heavier than the Elise. Without enough space, engineers had to lengthen the chassis. The weight distribution was different. The car failed all crash tests, so it was back to the design phase.

"It is kind of like if you bought a house," Musk said, "and it's not the house you want, but you figure you can just make it into the house you want. But you end up throwing out everything except for one wall and the basement. It would have been way cheaper just to level it."

In 2008, Musk renegotiated supplier contracts, slashed costs, fired 30 percent of Tesla's staff, and closed the Detroit office. He began looking for alternative sources of revenue and began manufacturing battery packs for Daimler's electric smart car, the Mercedes A-Class, and Toyota's electric RAV4. He applied for a government loan guarantee, arguing that bailout funds shouldn't be limited to makers of gas-guzzlers. Making the case that a small electric car company deserved government assistance, he received a $465 million loan from the U.S. government to fund the next-generation Tesla Model S sedan.

"If you're a founder or CEO, you have to do all kinds of tasks you might not want to do. Nothing is too menial," Musk said. "If you don't do your chores, the company won't succeed. You've got to do whatever it takes." A young Tesla employee recalled the time when Musk climbed up to get behind the wheel of a vehicle stuck on the production line, then backed it off the platform as factory workers wondered what to do.

Musk spends Tuesday through Thursday at Tesla and the rest of the week at SpaceX, serving as CEO of both startups. Eighteen months after he stepped in at Tesla, the company built the first production vehicle to use lithium-ion battery cells and get more than 200 miles per charge.

In June 2010, Musk took Tesla Motors public as the first automotive IPO since Ford Motor Company issued stock in 1956. "You don't want to own this stock! You don't want to lease it! You shouldn't even rent the darn thing!" ranted *Mad Money*'s Jim Cramer. Yet four years after issuing into the public markets, Tesla Motors stock has continued to increase in value. Musk surprised critics again.

And in 2013, the Model S was named Motor Trend Car of the Year, the first car with a noncombustion engine to take the prize. The sleek sedan is an engineering marvel. Yet Tesla remains a fledgling startup in the auto industry. Traditional auto manufacturers dwarf it in size.

Musk brought Tesla back from the brink. But it was not without angst.

"I worry a lot about failure," Musk said as we walked the Tesla factory floor. "Yeah, absolutely. I feel fear quite strongly."

As I watched huge sheets of aluminum being delicately stamped, cut, and folded into the Model S's frame, and giant red-and-black robots install windows and connect wires with a precision touch, it seemed difficult to imagine this company had struggled just a few years ago. So how did Musk persevere?

"If something is important enough, or you *believe* that something is important enough, even if you are scared, you still keep going," he said.

It's easier to accept setbacks when you are convinced your work matters. Creators are passionate about what they do, and that devotion allows them to endure hardships that come their way.

"Does what I'm doing count? Is it okay if I fail? The answer is yes, I'm sure," Stella & Dot founder Jessica Herrin said. "There can be business initiatives about which I can say, 'Uh, it may or may not work out,' but my compass is pointing in the right direction. Is what I'm doing for the right reasons? It has to be always yes." Herrin describes building a business that empowers women as her calling.

"There are no guarantees," Opower cofounder Alex Laskey said. In 2013, Laskey discovered he had a brain tumor pressing on his cranial nerve. It was benign, but the experience prompted him to reevaluate his life. "I'd like to be a better husband and a better son. I'm a pretty good dad. In terms of my work," he added, "I feel uncomplicated about it. That's a very good way to feel. I can't imagine spending my time doing something purposeless."

Elon Musk said, "Sustainable energy is a problem that must get solved." He wrote papers in college about the importance of electric cars and solar power. "My mom has the studies," he said with a laugh. "I'm not making it up! It's not like somebody told me to invent the story afterward." The survival of Tesla Motors illustrates Musk's passion for his work.

Sometimes, failures can be humbling. Just ask Netflix cofounder Reed Hastings. "I messed up," Hastings wrote on the Netflix blog in September 2011. "In hindsight, I slid into arrogance based upon past success."

A few months earlier, Hastings had announced that Netflix would split itself into two businesses: a DVD-by-mail company and a streaming online video service, each charging $7.99 a month. The ill-fated effort to hike prices led to fury among subscribers—some 800,000 angry customers canceled service, and there were calls for his resignation—and put Netflix into a death spiral.

On October 10, 2011, Hastings reversed his decision. The DVD-by-mail service would remain part of Netflix.

Only a year before, *Fortune* magazine had named him Business Person of the Year; now, media criticism included an ongoing *Saturday Night Live* parody. Netflix's stock price plummeted from just under $300 a share to about $53 in September 2012, wiping out almost $12 billion of value.

Hastings wasn't certain that Netflix could recover, but he didn't panic. He maintained his long-term vision for the streaming business and focused on delivering better service to existing customers, including DVD-by-mail subscribers.

"We weren't going to find an idea or gesture that would make people love us again overnight. We had to earn their trust by being very steady and disciplined," he said.

"He dusted himself off, stood back up, and started running," said Richard Greenfield, a media analyst at financial services firm BTIG. "Very few people can do that."

In 2012, Netflix added nearly ten million streaming subscribers. In 2013, it began to offer original programming with *House of Cards* and *Orange Is the New Black* as a way to provide more value to subscribers. Later that year, for the first time, Netflix earned more than $1 billion in quarterly revenue. By the end of 2013, the company passed forty million subscribers worldwide, of whom approximately thirty million were streaming customers. Despite the waning DVD-by-mail business, Netflix surpassed HBO in number of subscribers.

YES . . . AND

Failing wisely is about moving through situations. Creators overcome setbacks and adjust on the fly. They improvise, reframe, and move forward. Most of us haven't learned to react seamlessly and not overthink failures. Creators move on quickly to focus on what comes next.

Improvisational comics perform without a script. They take risks and adapt in the moment. It is very similar to how creators react in a changing environment, building new ideas without knowing what will work.

The first rule of improv is to say "yes . . . and." Each comedian first needs to agree and accept reality, the way it is. By saying yes, she accepts the situation. But the act can't move forward without additional information: hence "and" followed by a contribution. "Yes . . . and" starts with an open mind and no fear. A "yes . . . and" response paves the way for the next move.

Consider this improvisational comedy example. One comedian begins by telling a story, offering a sentence or two outlining the premise, something like. "Heard your house guest got locked out last night." The next comedian accepts the premise and adds to it: "Yes! . . . And she got doused by the sprinkler as she tried to get in." The conversation builds with "Yep . . . And turns out she fit through the doggie door." With "yes . . . and," the story builds as the comedians craft something entertaining.

Improv actors accept the premise, even if it is not particularly good, and aim to improve upon it. Good improv comedians do this seamlessly, injecting joke after joke. If one bit doesn't work, they don't reject it. Rather than worry about the parts that don't work, the performers simply let the story unfold.

This framework is valuable for creators. The ability to accept reality as is and build on the context, whether it is in a comedy club with an eager audience or in a market hungry for new products and ideas, is critical to success. Whether they are programmers in Silicon Valley or former athletes promoting the latest athletic wear, creators must possess the drive and confidence to respond positively and build on what came before.

The idea of "yes . . . and" is to avoid suppressing ideas or being afraid to share them, even if they are questionable. If creators are on the right track, they succeed. If not, they develop something better. By thinking quickly and maintaining an open mind, improvisational comedians and creators float all sorts of ideas with confidence, knowing some will succeed while others will fall short.

The real value in improvisation is that it allows creators to try new ideas without fear of failure. It requires astute observation, quick thinking, and an ability to move rapidly to the next idea without forgetting what was learned. Creators entertain new ideas, understanding that many will fail, just as improv comedians jump from joke to joke, knowing that not all will make audiences laugh. Creators are willing to say "yes . . . and," keeping themselves receptive to fresh ideas. It is a way of failing wisely.

TURN SETBACKS INTO STRENGTH

David Neeleman, cofounder of JetBlue, was not diagnosed with attention deficit disorder (ADD) until he was an adult. As a child, he had struggled in school and been cast as an outsider. Isolated and different, he couldn't succeed on a traditional track and dropped out of college. That difficult beginning would be more than enough to shut down the best of us, but Neeleman forged ahead, again and again.

Over the course of his career, Neeleman has founded three successful airlines, each a trailblazer, and each time, he could have been counted out. When he was twenty-three, his first company—a travel booking business—failed after the airline he was working with filed for bankruptcy. So Neeleman tried again. Nine years later, after selling his company Morris Air to Southwest Airlines, he was dismissed by his mentor, Southwest's Herb Kelleher. He got back up. On his third try, as cofounder and CEO of JetBlue, the company's board fired him after the so-called Valentine's Day Massacre, a February

14, 2007, snowstorm that stranded thousands of JetBlue passengers. Yet again, he managed to bounce back. Neeleman went on to found today's fastest-growing airline in Brazil, Azul—the Portuguese word for blue.

"Having ADD, it drives me crazy to fly," Neeleman said. "And I can still remember the exact spot in the office where JetBlue vice president Tom Anderson walked in and said, 'Hey, I got this brochure about a company in Florida that's doing live television on corporate jets.' I said, 'That's it!'" Neeleman's natural restlessness allowed him to see the benefit of additional in-flight stimulation for JetBlue customers. He immediately flew to Florida and cut a deal that put JetBlue in the entertainment business.

In 1999, Neeleman had raised $125 million to start JetBlue, the largest investment in the history of airlines, to "bring humanity to air travel." He eliminated first-class seats from JetBlue's planes to give everyone more leg room and installed leather seating that cost twice as much but would last twice as long. He chose Airbus to manufacture planes because the competition was flying narrower Boeing jets, thereby gaining an extra inch in width and two inches more in legroom for each passenger. Vowing never to overbook, JetBlue would not sell more tickets than seats, a common practice in the industry.

Known as Mr. JetBlue, Neeleman flew on the airline at least once a week. He would walk the aisles passing out snacks and soliciting feedback, help clean the aircraft after landing, and sometimes unload luggage with baggage handlers. He made a practice of sitting in the very last row to demonstrate that pleasing the customer was more important than pleasing the CEO. It worked. JetBlue took off. The airline was profitable by its third full quarter and went public in 2002.

Then came the unexpected East Coast blizzard of 2007. Icy weather grounded flights. Still, controllers sent aircraft to the runway. Some flights were stranded on the tarmac at New York's JFK Airport for ten hours. Cancellations of some 1,700 flights over the next five days stranded more than 130,000 passengers, infuriating customers and exposing organizational failings.

Neeleman tried to navigate the carrier through the crisis. He spent three days living on two hours of sleep per night working from the airline's operation center. He quickly realized that "we weren't capable of putting Humpty Dumpty back together again in an expeditious fashion," he said. The proper decision-making infrastructure was not in place to coordinate planes, pilots, and passengers. "It started on a Thursday, and by Monday, we were back up to full speed, but the damage had been done," he conceded.

JetBlue's reputation crashed. The customer-centric airline was tarnished. Planes from other airlines were on the tarmac just as long, but customers expected more from JetBlue.

Neeleman took responsibility and gave twenty-seven media interviews the day after the incident—beginning with NBC's *Today* in the morning and ending with CBS's *Late Show* at 11:30 p.m. He made a heartfelt apology on YouTube, asking customers to trust the airline again. He created the Passenger Bill of Rights, pledging travel vouchers to inconvenienced customers. Neeleman also drafted a twenty-two-point plan to overhaul operations of the company. He promised to revamp JetBlue's reservation system, triple the size of the carrier's operations control staff, and train 1,300 nonairport workers to help in bad-weather emergencies, among other fixes.

"It didn't save my job, but JetBlue bounced back quickly, and we did right by our customers," Neeleman told me. Three months later, the JetBlue board unceremoniously ousted Neeleman. It was determined that the company needed a CEO in better control of operations. "Just months before, I had my highest CEO evaluations of my entire time at JetBlue," he said.

Not one to let grass grow beneath his feet, he bounced back. "I left JetBlue in May of 2007, and we launched our first flight at Azul in December," Neeleman recalled. He exported the JetBlue model to Brazil, vowing to make this one even better. No reason to wait around.

A large part of a creator's success is an ability to retool and look ahead. "It was good to bury myself in something else, something great for Brazil," Neeleman said. "I also think there probably was a little competitive spirit at work. I'm going to drive Azul to have a higher market cap than JetBlue, and it's going to be a better airline. We're going to show these guys that side by side, in every metric, we're doing better."

Creators don't expend energy on past failures. They learn and take the lessons forward. "It's really not about what happens to you in life; it's about how you deal with it," Neeleman said. "You move on. I've got 10,000 crew members in Brazil and twenty-five million Brazilian customers this year who are thrilled with the JetBlue board. They'd all send them a thank-you note if they could."

During my research, creators described setbacks—learning disabilities, family losses, professional dead ends, and financial blows—that made them find alternative ways around problems.

Segway inventor Dean Kamen never graduated from college. "I'm undegreed, but I don't consider myself uneducated," Kamen said. And the Segway was considered a flop, a professional embarrassment when first launched. "If you really want to succeed at things that other people haven't done yet, you have to get good at failing," Kamen explained. "You have to get comfortable with failing and not let it destroy you intellectually or emotionally. You work hard at something you're passionate about, and you never give up."

127

Gavin Newsom, cofounder of hospitality company Plump-Jack Group, today the lieutenant governor of California, described his struggle to learn in a traditional way: "I couldn't succeed in school, given my dyslexia, so I had to find what I was good at—entrepreneurship and politics. I could work through people in another way."

These creators join a long list of entrepreneurs who attribute success to an ability to overcome setbacks and persevere. Creators maneuver their way around problems. They overcome weaknesses with improvised solutions.

Carol Dweck, a psychology professor at Stanford University, has conducted research indicating that individuals can grow through adversity. Her work demonstrates that people tend to lean toward one of two general ways of thinking about their abilities. Those favoring a "fixed mindset," as Dweck calls it, believe that intelligence and abilities are set, that we have innate talents and fixed traits. Those favoring a "growth mindset," on the other hand, believe that intelligence and abilities can be grown through effort, that we can follow our passions to develop our capabilities. Creators cultivate a growth mindset.

"When confronted with a task, people with a fixed mindset ask 'Am I going to be good at it immediately?'" Dweck explained when we met in her Stanford office. "Whereas those with a growth mindset ask, 'Well, can I learn to do it?'" Fixed mindsets lead individuals to be overly concerned with validation, in forms such as grades, titles, status, and recognition. They become afraid of mistakes, since setbacks tarnish their reputations. They gravitate to activities that validate their abilities. Growth mindset individuals, by contrast, view setbacks as opportunities for growth. Instead of staying in their comfort zone, they seek activities that expand their skills and venture out, believing they can grow into their potential by trying new things.

It is not simply an issue of either you have it or you don't, Dweck said. An individual's mindset can be influenced by what she believes is more important: ability or effort. In one of Dweck's largest studies, conducted with four hundred fifth graders in New York City, students received a set of puzzles. One group was praised for their ability and told, "Wow, you got a huge number correct. That's a really good score. You must be smart. You are very good at this." Others were praised for their effort: "You must have worked very hard." When given a subsequent round of puzzles, students could choose either an easier or a more difficult challenge. The experiment revealed that the majority of those praised for their intelligence chose the easier task, but 90 percent of students who had been praised for their effort chose the challenging task.

In the next round, students were given harder problems on which they wouldn't be able to perform as well. Afterward, they were told they had done worse and were asked for their reactions. Students who had been praised for their intelligence had their confidence shaken. They refused to take the problems home to work out, and 40 percent went so far as to lie about their score to improve it. These students viewed failure as an embarrassment to be avoided. But the students who had been praised for their effort said they liked the more difficult task despite the struggle. They performed better than those who had been praised for their intelligence and, in fact, opted to continue to work on the puzzles at home.

Dweck's research shows how we can grow through failure and how praising effort encourages individuals, whereas praising ability alone reduces persistence. Individuals can learn to see setbacks as opportunities to start again, with more information. Creators master this. They reframe mistakes as opportunities to grow instead of viewing them as trapdoors to failure. They remind themselves of situations in which they have confronted setbacks and persevered, and they build resilience knowing they can get smarter, learn new things, and stretch beyond weaknesses.

WHAT'S WORTH DOING EVEN IF YOU'RE AFRAID?

Are you spending your time pursuing your best idea? If your work suddenly were to end, would others miss your contribution?

Building breakout businesses isn't easy. Nearly every creator I interviewed described uncomfortable moments, staring down fear, and making the decision to persevere. Many told a story of having their back up against the wall, then somehow overcoming seemingly insurmountable odds to push forward.

In 1999, Alexander Asseily and Hosain Rahman founded a consumer technology company called Aliph, later renamed Jawbone, to build an innovative noise-canceling Bluetooth headset. It didn't launch until 2007. "There was basically one thing that convinced me to keep going when we had been through years of roller coaster rides," Asseily said. "That was the realization that if I didn't, I was convinced enough in the vision that someone else would prove it, and I would regret it forever and ever."

Asseily describes 2005 and 2006 as the "nuclear winter" for Jawbone, fighting through problem after problem to launch the startup's long-awaited initial product. "I knew it was going to be painful for a couple more years. We were just forced out of circumstance to be very, very focused," he said. Asseily worked from a factory in China, testing headset sound quality on thousands of units, subsisting for weeks on fried rice. Finally, the first batch of 10,000 units shipped—despite Jawbone's inability to pay the manufacturer on time. When the headsets arrived on the East Coast, the warehouse was closed. It was a few days before Christmas. By coincidence, Asseily had met the CEO of the distribution company on a ferry in Hong Kong weeks before. He sent a text message asking for help in getting the shipment inside the Maryland storage facility. The CEO responded: It will be done.

"I think something happens when you get into this mode of 'I'm going to keep going no matter what,'" Asseily told me. "Things align themselves to make magic happen. It wasn't just that time."

Creators have the ability to make a right turn, left turn, or U-turn, and start again when circumstances dictate. While failure is not fun or easy, the vast majority of failures are surmountable. The biggest failure of all would be refusing to try.

Chapter 5

NETWORK MINDS

Alone we can do so little; together we can do so much.

—Helen Keller

In November 2011, Jawbone launched the UP, a half-inch-wide rubberized health-tracking bracelet. It was the first wristband with an internal computer, designed to be small, beautiful, and functional. The UP promised to help improve the wearer's health by measuring everything from sleep patterns to steps taken to calories burned. It was to become part of the user's life, wearable 24 hours a day. The product was a sensation, selling out immediately.

Just three weeks after the UP launched, however, customers reported frustrations with charging and syncing the device. In some cases, it shut down completely.

Jawbone didn't cut its losses and shelve the product. Quite the opposite. Company founders Hosain Rahman and Alexander Asseily reached out to find a solution.

As CEO, Rahman acknowledged the problem on the company's Web site and offered a full refund, no questions asked. "We are so committed to this product that we're offering you the option of using it for free," he wrote. Giving customers the option to get their money back *and* keep the product built trust and invited feedback.

Then Rahman assembled a war room bringing together experts from engineering, manufacturing, design, data analytics, marketing, and customer service to discover what had gone wrong and redesign the bracelet from scratch. They papered walls with flowcharts and product design diagrams and mapped out potential problems, dissecting every angle. The task was especially difficult given the UP's many distinct functions.

Over the next twelve months, Jawbone consumed 16,000 man hours of labor, passing through 200 hardware designs, forty-six weeks of user trials, and 2.9 million hours of real-world user testing as it worked to improve the product. Every component of the UP was analyzed, down to the construction of its capacitors. In December 2012, the UP relaunched and became a breakout success, surging ahead of competitors Nike FuelBand and Fitbit.

How did the Jawbone founders catapult out of a tricky situation to build the company's greatest product success?

They networked minds.

COGNITIVE DIVERSITY

It's the difference in how we think, what perspectives we bring to a problem, and the steps we take to tackle difficult challenges that, when combined, unlock breakthrough results. Creators network minds to tap varied perspectives. This powerful act delivers novel solutions.

Each of us organizes information our own way. When we rely on our knowledge to solve problems, psychologists call it "local search." We sift through our experiences to devise solutions. When faced with issues, we rarely deviate from past approaches. Cultural anthropologists call the phenomenon of organizing information "pile sorting." We categorize data into our unique piles.

Creators build on each other's ideas to overcome these constraints. They harness cognitive diversity by assembling all kinds of thinkers. We often think of diversity in terms of our race, ethnicity, age, gender, or socioeconomic status. Cognitive diversity, however, refers to what goes on inside our heads: how we interpret a situation, categorize information, and envision a set of possibilities.

The famous Bletchley Park code-breaking squad assembled by British intelligence during World War II provides a dramatic example. To crack what was called the Nazi Enigma code, individuals came together from across the Allied forces: English, Americans, Poles, Aussies, and others, all with diverse skills. They gathered clandestinely in Room 40 at the Bletchley Park estate, about fifty miles northwest of London, and launched what today we would call the ultimate hack-a-thon. Language experts, military strategists, mathematicians, engineers, cryptographers, historians, philosophers, classicists, even crossword puzzle aficionados, worked feverishly to decipher encrypted messages that would reveal German military moves and intelligence. Their success was crucial to halting and then reversing the German advance in Europe and North Africa. In Winston Churchill's words, it was "the goose that laid the golden egg."

At Bletchley Park, networking minds was an urgent priority: the effort saved thousands of lives. More and more, endeavors of all kinds require this skill. Research shows that management teams are more innovative when they leverage a wide range of perceptions. Engineers with differing experiences achieve greater performance, and diverse boards of directors make better decisions.

Creators hone the ability to bring together unlikely allies, breaking away from industry standards to solve problems in radical ways. To thwart terrorist networks, Palantir Technologies founders Peter Thiel, Alex Karp, Joe Lonsdale, Stephen Cohen, and Nathan Gettings team some of the most talented software engineers of Silicon Valley with analysts from various government intelligence agencies to design a software tool to tag and decipher previously unintelligible information. To build a reusable rocket at SpaceX, Elon Musk draws on minds as varied as NASA engineers, thermodynamics physicists, navigational software programmers, and business managers. Dean Kamen runs an interdisciplinary lab at DEKA Research and Development with 400 interdisciplinary engineers, scientists, and medical experts that has invented the Segway, Slingshot portable water-purification system, and iBot wheelchair.

When we encounter problems, we don't know where we will find the answer. Our differences in experience, education, personality, and other traits help teams devise solutions from various angles.

Even the best and brightest rely on networking minds. Nobel Prizes awarded in recent years increasingly honor teams, not solo scientists. From 2004 to 2013, for example, seven of the ten Nobel Prizes in chemistry were awarded to two or three scientists, making twenty-three recipients in all for the decade, whereas from 1901 to 1910, each prize went to one individual. Some critics want to reevaluate rules restricting Nobel Prizes to three recipients or fewer. The 2011 physics prize, for example, was awarded to three astronomers who were part of two teams that discovered that the expansion of the universe is accelerating. Hundreds of scientists worked together to arrive at this conclusion. "If something is discovered at CERN, and there are 3,000 people in the collaboration, what are we going to do then?" asked Lars Bergström, secretary of the Nobel Committee for Physics, referring to the European center for scientific research in Switzerland.

The era of lone geniuses is ending. Issues today are far too interconnected to be tackled by a single individual, and no one person can synthesize all the information around us. Whether building a technology, organic food company, or fashion business, creators network minds to devise solutions. They harness cognitive diversity by developing forums where diverse minds can mingle. To do this, they create the commons, foster flash teams, catalyze prize competitions, and use game mechanics to solve problems in innovative ways.

CREATE THE COMMONS

"If you find unique ways to pull disciplines together, you open up experiences for people," Rahman said. "You solve problems that people didn't even know they had and build products they couldn't live without."

After Hosain Rahman and Alexander Asseily founded a company in 1999 to develop artificial intelligence software, they changed directions and developed noise-canceling software and a headset to house it. "We weren't signal-processing guys, but we found the right scientists, and we knew how to synthesize," Rahman said. The Jawbone Bluetooth headset became the biggest breakthrough in mobile audio processing in thirty years. Then, in 2011, they built the JAMBOX, a wireless speaker that integrates audio technology with smartphone music players. It transformed the category. With the UP, the Jawbone founders had a different proposition—to design a wearable health tracker that would work with a mobile lifestyle without looking like "geekware." The ability to integrate hardware and software to create complex, simple-to-use, and aesthetically appealing technology requires creating a commons—a space where people can build on each other's ideas.

"Apple created the tip of an era, and we are coming right behind them," Rahman said when we met at Jawbone's headquarters in San Francisco's Design District. "Bringing design and engineering together is hard to do. It's expensive. It's time consuming."

Hardware people don't naturally think about iteration. They use expensive materials and have product cycles that can take years of development, and they think in terms of creating a perfected product before it goes out the door. Software designers, by contrast, push products into the world to see what happens and rapidly refine prototypes. Jawbone also integrates design. Chief creative officer Yves Béhar, founder of design agency Fuseproject, and his team aim to create devices that are beautiful, natural feeling, and intuitive to use. "It's a lot of mashing and smashing and getting people to map out every single part of any particular product, identify friction points, and think of ways to resolve them," Rahman explained.

Jawbone's products combine intricate hardware and easy-to-use software. Building both hardware devices and software programs is rare among technology companies—especially startups. But Jawbone has enjoyed great success.

The UP wristband incorporates sophisticated motion sensors to track micro-movements that indicate sleep patterns; it then vibrates to wake users at the optimal time. It measures exercise intensity and allows users to track food choices by scanning a barcode or searching a database for nutritional information. It also provides a visual tracking report of activity in an iOS app interface and integrates social features to help users compare health goals and accomplishments with those of friends.

Wearable computing devices heighten design and engineering

complexity and require designers to think about the overall consumer experience. When people drop a smartphone, they realize it might get damaged. They don't consider hard knocks a threat to wristbands.

"We came up with a flexible rubber band that had a computer inside stretched out through the length of the wristband," Asseily said. "No one had ever built anything like it, but we underestimated how people would bend it in ways that twist the circuit board and wash dishes wearing it, combining hot water and detergent that affected the band's porosity and internal components."

Jawbone had tested the UP intensively before its release, but the company had underestimated the stress it would undergo: Children tugged at the bracelets when playing with their parents, users spilled Jack Daniel's on it during a night on the town, and a glitch in a capacitor on the charging circuit rendered the battery useless when warm water, combined with shampoo, penetrated the wristband's watertight seals.

To solve the problem, Jawbone conducted what it calls one of the largest ethnographic studies imaginable. "We crowdsourced honest behavior," Asseily said. "We had a population of people who were willing to live with the slightly imperfect product and help us make it better." Beta testers wore the device for nearly three million hours. All companies test products, but Jawbone networked minds with users on a massive scale to obtain feedback and design a truly wearable device.

To fix the UP, the company developed new molding processes that created a protective layer around the internal circuitry and redistributed electronics to make the internal band more flexible. The band was treated with a bonding agent to reduce friction against clothing and prevent snags that would pull the bracelet. Software was updated with greater functionality for the smartphone app. The experience illustrated the value of networking minds.

"Bringing in great minds from both Massive Health and Visere will help us to develop software that's both simple and beautiful and build the very best integrated hardware, software, and data platform in the world," Rahman said when Jawbone acquired these two software companies to upgrade its diet and health-tracking technology. In 2013, Jawbone went even further and acquired BodyMedia, a company that tracks health through body sensor data points and can run clinical trials with hospitals. "We gained a team that was world class at multisensors," Rahman said.

"This is the future of computing," Rahman asserted. "It's gone from the size of your desk, to your bag, to your pocket, to your wrist. Next, these things are going to have sensors that talk to your thermostat and tell it how hot or cold you are." In fact, not long after we met, Jawbone announced a partnership with Nest that connects its devices to thermostats.

While the technology will continue to change, the means to improve it will remain the same: by networking minds.

Knowing that multidisciplinary teams using a variety of technology platforms are the future of work, creators design physical and virtual spaces where people can build on each other's ideas.

Radical collaboration finds a home at the d.school, the Hasso Plattner Institute of Design at Stanford University. "Never before had there been an opera singer with an anthropologist and a geologist with a physicist on the same team," said David Kelley, cofounder of the d.school and the design firm IDEO.

Conceived as a "school crossing," or hub, the d.school allows diverse students to practice interdisciplinary innovation. No degrees are awarded, but courses fill up quickly. Something of an anomaly for academia, the d.school fosters a collaborative approach to solving problems.

"We play this team sport," Kelley told me. "You'll notice around here, vertical spaces are all writable." He points to messy whiteboards as an invitation to contribute ideas, and he describes how students gather data, build prototypes, identify what works, then start again. "In a team sport, you have to move your arms, because you have to show three or four people your work at the same time," Kelley said. "If you happen to have an individual score, you'll have a desk, but if you are going to talk to three other people, you can't do it at a desk. It doesn't work."

Everything at the d.school is on wheels and can be reconfigured in about fifteen minutes. Whiteboards mounted on Z-racks can be moved to create shared space, allowing teams to map ideas. Teams can move walls and use a truss system to arrange sliding panels to create studios for specific needs. In a two-hour class, a space might be reconfigured to modules for lectures, projects, debriefing, interviews, and prototyping. Varying layouts promotes the ability to network minds.

I watched students sketch diagrams and move colored sticky notes from wall to wall. In a prototyping lab, engineers, business students, poets, and doctors tasked with improving the security screening experience at airports glued cardboard pieces together. Teams created a mock product. The steps were a rough outline of general processes involved in "design thinking," which relies heavily on collaboration and feedback to generate solutions.

"It's my life's work to get people who have different backgrounds to be able to build on each other's ideas," Kelley said. He sat on a tall stool, surrounded by Styrofoam prototypes, stacks of green chairs, and a bright red couch.

Kelley is bald and has a Groucho Marx look, minus the cigar: thick black mustache, heavy black glasses. An unassuming figure usually dressed in jeans, flannel shirt, and dark tennis shoes with colored laces, he could be mistaken for a quirky professor instead of one of the world's foremost product designers.

Kelley grew up in Dayton, Ohio, in a family of tire makers. He had no exposure to design, but he tinkered. He "improved" the family washing machine, though it never washed another load of clothes. He dismantled the piano: His mother still sends him parts, hoping he will find a way to reassemble it. Trained as an engineer, he worked for Boeing, analyzing lighting systems for the 747 aircraft, and later for National Cash Register, designing circuit boards.

In 1978, Kelley, along with Dean Hovey, rented office space for $90 per month above a dress shop in Palo Alto, California. There they launched a fledgling firm that would go on to create the Nike wraparound sunglasses, the mechanical whale in the movie *Free Willy*, fishing rods for kids, and, most innovative of all, the original Apple computer mouse. That company today is called IDEO.

As a builder of so many creations, Kelley learned to draw on other minds for help. "If you are talking about an idea, no one helps you," he said. "But the minute you bring a prototype in the room, everyone is ready to tell you what is wrong with it, and they can help you build and build and build." At the d.school, students prototype ideas to draw as much input as possible. They glue scraps of paper together, act out a process through skits, or make a video to engage others with their ideas. It is not the prototype that matters so much as the ability to harness the collective brainpower of diverse people.

"You don't have to prototype everything," Kelley told me, "just the part that's not believable. So if I said I had this machine that can move across the floor and then levitate you, I don't have to prototype the move-across-the-floor part; but the levitate part, I should probably prove that." Prototypes help creators gather feedback from people who would use it or hate it, experts who know about it, and novices who tinker with the idea and improve it.

Creators believe everyone has something to offer. The sociologist's observation is as important as the engineer's input. Respect for each voice is necessary; remaining open to others' points of view is critical.

"Sometimes you have an insight because of culture," Kelley said. "In Japan, you pull the car up anywhere and pull the gas pump down from overhead to the car. That's not our system! We have to get the car close up to the curb. I wouldn't come up with the overhead thing"—he waves his arms as if pulling down a gas nozzle—"but the Japanese person would!"

In an effort to create a commons that invite all perspectives, d.school faculty "try to level out the status between professor and students," Kelley said. Three professors teach each course, and students come from each of Stanford's seven graduate schools. The richness of the conversation helps everyone feel equal.

You can't control creative problem solving, so how do you direct something when you aren't looking for a specific outcome? "Creativity follows space," said George Kembel, cofounder and global director of the d.school, as we walked through the school's garage door entrance. Kembel described how creativity flows like music. Music resonates most in the venue where it is meant to be played. Gregorian chants, for example, would be lost in a stadium, and hiphop would sound out of place in a cathedral. The feel of a dive bar, however, is perfect for blues bands and indie rockers. The same logic applies to designing space to encourage problem solving.

Space can be designed to provoke action. The d.school works to maintain a culture that encourages students to get up and try something, to test their ideas. "We make the seating uncomfortable intentionally," Kembel said. "We don't want students to be stuck in their chairs." This is contrary to the typical business landscape since the birth of the office cubicle in 1968.

"If space is 'not precious,' people can hack it," Kembel said. "If it's too fancy, they won't have a sense of ownership or feel safe to make changes." The d.school started in a trailer on the Stanford campus and moved three times in its first six years. That taught the d.school founders how unfinished space encourages a work-in-progress mentality.

Part of networking minds effectively is defining the process. Learning to work in concert requires attention to interpersonal dynamics. If one person is trying to generate options and another is trying to prioritize feedback while a third is trying to focus on the team and a fourth is trying to press toward a resolution, teams can implode. Clarifying the team's work at a given moment keeps diverse minds in sync: "Now we are generating options; next we are experimenting; then we converge on a decision." At different times, team members can play to their various strengths, as opposed to having a designated leader throughout.

Out of the d.school have come several thriving enterprises. Akshay Kothari and Ankit Gupta, graduate students in electrical engineering and computer science, respectively, started a daily news application as a project in a d.school course in 2010. They had experienced frustration keeping up on the news and observed others "getting flustered and stressed out using Google Reader, opening it to messages that read something like 'You missed 1,000 stories since you last logged on,'" Kothari recalled. In a ten-week d.school course, they set out to develop an iPad app that would make it easy to stay on top of news headlines and browse stories visually.

Working from a café in Palo Alto, Kothari and Gupta—both introverted and self-described geeks—tested early versions on coffee-sipping customers reading the news. The iPad had just debuted, making it a novelty that Kothari and Gupta used to attract passers-by and gain valuable input. Arriving every morning at nine, they interacted with everyday readers to understand where they struggled with the app. These creators observed what happened when readers were unable to find something, why they had difficulty closing an article, or how they hit snags attempting to browse another headline. They made hundreds of small changes every day to adjust a button, color, or display. As Kothari and Gupta improved their prototype, they asked café patrons to point out flaws. "In two weeks, we went from people saying, 'This looks awful,' to asking, 'Is this app pre-loaded on the iPad?'" Kothari said. The result became Pulse News, an application that aggregates news from publishing sources ranging from the *Wall Street Journal* and Huffington Post to ESPN, BBC News, and *Time*.

A few weeks later, Steve Jobs unexpectedly heralded the Pulse News app from the main stage of the Apple Worldwide Developers Conference. Since then, more than thirty million people have downloaded Pulse. The ability to network minds with café patrons as Kothari and Gupta built the product made it possible for these creators to design an app that fit readers' needs. "We've been really blessed to have this opportunity," Kothari told me. "It's amazing for me to work on something that I can give to my grandparents in India, who never before had a computer, and now they read local and international news every day on an iPad." In 2013, Kothari and Gupta sold Pulse to LinkedIn for $90 million.

Doug Dietz, the executive behind GE Healthcare's magnetic resonance imaging (MRI) equipment, also learned about the power of networking minds at the d.school, where he enrolled in an executive education program. Dietz had won awards for his industrial design of General Electric's scanning equipment. He had come to a hospital to watch one of his machines in action when he encountered a seven-year-old girl and her anxious parents on their way to an appointment. When the family turned the corner and the girl saw the MRI machine, she began crying and screaming.

Dietz realized that during the years he had been designing these machines, he had never asked, "What's the experience like for a child?" He drove home frustrated. "I just remember thinking that I failed at my job," he admitted. He had built a powerful medical device, but the beneficiaries weren't just technologists and doctors. Dietz needed to design this technology for patients, especially children, who would lie inside the machine.

So Dietz assembled childhood experts from Milwaukee's Betty Brinn Children's Museum and child life specialists from Children's Hospital of Pittsburgh of the University of Pittsburgh Medical Center, as well as nurses, technologists, and radiologists, leaders of a local day-care center, and GE engineering and manufacturing designers, to help him consider how to improve the experience for children. He listened as kids talked about going to camp, dressing up like a big sister, dreaming about rocket ships to space. Dietz realized that his job wasn't just to design a scanner. It was to turn a medical device into an adventure for kids.

"I pulled together this crazy cross-functional team that helped me get to some of the magic of the Adventure Series," Dietz said. "In order to look at this from a bigger picture and really make a difference, I had to get more people involved."

He covered the MRI scanner with colorful decals that suggested a journey to outer space or a jungle safari, and designed scan rooms around related themes, complete with music that created a friendly environment for kids. Before their scans, children receive a backpack with a cartoon book about going to camp and then are greeted by a "camp counselor" instead of a nurse. Dietz produced nine different themes, each of which makes the procedure feel more like an adventure.

Eighty percent of children who entered GE's old MRI scanners, including the girl Dietz first encountered, had to be sedated. But for

Dietz's redesigned Adventure Series scanner, the percentage of children needing sedation is near zero. Patient satisfaction has increased 90 percent, and efficiency is up by 70 percent. The redesign enables parents, children, and medical professionals to address important health problems with less stress and better results. Dietz even overheard a little girl ask her mother, "Can we come back tomorrow?" Networking minds worked.

THE PAIN IS WORTH THE GAIN

We understand that people from different cultural, gender, and professional backgrounds bring unique perspectives that can help unlock solutions. When we add an anthropologist to a group of computer scientists, or Chinese people to a group of Nordics, we assume that the outsiders will be the ones who produced unexpected perspectives. Networking minds, however, comes with a counterintuitive benefit. The surprising truth is that working with people who are "different" improves our own performance.

In diverse environments, we are primed to expect that unusual information will come out and we're therefore more likely to be motivated to express our own unique point of view. "People are not clones of each other," said Katherine Phillips, a professor of leadership and ethics at Columbia Business School. "We all have differences of opinion, and heterogeneous groups allow new knowledge to come forward."

Phillips's research demonstrates that by engaging with diverse minds, we become more alert to information, more open to reevaluating our own assumptions, and more attuned to solving the task. The act of networking minds prompts us to set aside traditional expectations and free ourselves to see things anew. Breakthrough insight can come not just from people who are "new" or "different" in a group, but from people who look the same but approach things from a different vantage point and will actually express a perspective otherwise left unsaid.

In groups where everyone looks the same, the norm is to not rock the boat. We often put social concerns ahead of voicing unique points of view. Psychologists have studied the need for belonging and observed that we want to be liked by people similar to ourselves. When we surround ourselves with dissimilar people, a social dynamic is created in which people have to explain why they agree or disagree with others. It may make us feel uneasy, but it pushes us to solve the problem at hand.

To test the effects of diversity on a group's problem-solving ability, Phillips conducted a study at Northwestern University with 242 members of four sororities and fraternities. Participants were asked to solve a fictitious murder mystery. Each was given a set of interviews conducted by a detective investigating a whodunit and had to decide on a suspect. To highlight social identity, large banners naming each sorority and fraternity hung in the test rooms, and participants were asked to sit with their "brothers" and "sisters" and wear name tags identifying their house.

Working independently, each person had twenty minutes to solve the murder. Individuals were asked to write a brief explanation of their choice. The participants were then assigned, based on their Greek affiliation as well as their choice of a suspect, to three-person teams. These three-person teams were given twenty minutes to compare notes and agree on a suspect. Five minutes into the deliberations, a fourth person joined the group. These new group members were either members of the same fraternity or sorority, or outsiders with a different Greek affiliation.

The groups with outsiders had less confidence in their decisions and reported that they were working less effectively than the homogeneous groups, yet they achieved superior results. Individually, the test subjects determined the actual murderer 44 percent of the time. Groups whose members belonged to the same fraternity or sorority solved the mystery 54 percent of the time, while diverse groups correctly identified the murderer 75 percent of the time, despite feelings of social discomfort.

"The pain is worth the gain," Phillips said. Although homogeneous groups found it more comfortable to work with those from the same fraternity or sorority, they became entrenched in their point of view and overconfident in their assumptions. Diverse groups, by contrast, experienced an upset of the status quo and felt insecure, but were motivated to reconcile opposite opinions. They were more focused and accurate. Even when newcomers agreed with one or more existing members of the group, individuals wanted to understand why someone "different" would hold the same point of view, and applied more focus to the task at hand.

Surrounding ourselves with people who are dissimilar often feels uncomfortable. "We don't like diversity because it makes us work harder," Phillips said. "We are cognitive misers and would rather not put forth so much effort if we don't have to, but discomfort serves a purpose."

Networking minds disrupts cohesion. By interacting with more diverse minds, creators move beyond routine thinking to come up with greater insights.

When we anticipate interacting with people who are "not like us," we come better prepared. In another study, by Phillips and her colleagues, each participant was asked his or her political affiliation before being given a similar fictitious murder mystery to solve: Someone who reached a different solution would then join that individual for a debate. Some participants were told that this person would agree with them politically, while others were told the person would hold an opposing political view. To display differences, researchers used party labels and color coding (red for Republicans, blue for Democrats).

Before debating their solutions, however, participants were asked to write down their arguments. These essays were scored for length, language, thoroughness, and robustness. Essays prepared by those who believed they would be debating someone with a different political bent were stronger, more thorough, and better reasoned than those written by participants who would debate a fellow thinker.

Phillips's study reveals that when we expect to engage with others with different points of view, we do our homework. We consider our argument and arrive better prepared, improving our own performance. Interacting with people not like us takes more work. As Phillips described it, "If you want big muscles, you have to go to the gym. It's painful."

But networking minds doesn't have to occur constantly. It can take the form of short bursts of project-based work. Creators quickly assemble "flash teams" to solve specific problems and address an urgent need.

FOSTER FLASH TEAMS

"Wham, this one's going to be big," Eric Rasmussen, founding CEO of Innovative Support to Emergencies, Diseases, and Disasters (In-STEDD), texted to Nicolás di Tada in Buenos Aires. Tada messaged back, "I am already on my way." Over the Virtual On-Site Operations Coordination Center, Gisli Olafsson sent a satellite telephone number and the message, "I'm arriving at 4:27."

In his day job, Olafsson worked for Microsoft Corporation. As a volunteer disaster responder, he flew from Reykjavík to Haiti following the 2010 earthquake there. His job was to track distress calls and direct the Icelandic rescue team.

In my research, I found examples of this kind of collective effort again and again. I call these groups flash teams. Enabled by technology, flash teams provide a new way to network minds to tackle all kinds of challenges. Flash teams come together quickly, go to work, then disband.

Rasmussen, a former Navy doctor, received word of the devastating 7.0 magnitude quake within five minutes of the initial tremor, and recognized immediately that the disaster would present an immense task. Seven minutes later, he had connected with seventy-five people in his worldwide first responders' network. Rasmussen and his flash team were assembled in Port-au-Prince within twelve hours. They were translating, mapping locations of victims, and rescuing survivors trapped under rubble.

Working alongside a scientist from the British Antarctic Survey team, Rasmussen set up an operations center to receive text messages, translate them from Creole to French or English, map locations on Google Earth, and deploy teams to rescue survivors. Desperate for news of loved ones, Haitians were jamming the networks of overwhelmed emergency centers, so InSTEDD and other flash-team responders installed infrastructure to intercept and manage more than 90,000 messages generated by the local population.

"A UN employee was trapped in a grocery store when it collapsed," Rasmussen said. "We got the message and circled it back. It was something like two and a half hours from the moment he sent it until the search team was on site. That's how good we got at this."

Rasmussen's Haiti team and others like it were made up of a diverse collection of elite responders from organizations as disparate as the American Red Cross, Tufts University, Google Earth, and the Icelandic rescuers. The teams saved hundreds of lives. Flash teams in first-response situations and search-and-rescue operations are born of urgent need; creators are just as likely to assemble project-specific teams to seize economic opportunities.

Working temporarily with diverse individuals is common in the motion-picture industry: actors, screenwriters, cinematographers, and directors have assembled and collaborated in this mode for years. Short-term, goal-oriented work also characterizes consulting firms. Legal teams assemble and reassemble within law firms case by case, just as mergers and acquisitions teams within investment banks work on specific financial deals. In hospitals, doctors, nurses, technicians, and social workers form shifting teams to treat patients individually.

Technology enables creators to form and disband teams on a project-to-project basis in much the same way. With mobile technology, social networking platforms, and other connectivity tools, people can come together for short periods as specialists and work intensively to solve a problem in which they share an interest.

Across my research, flash teams point to the future of work. One in three working Americans, an estimated forty-two million people, do not have jobs in the traditional sense, according to federal statistics dating back to 2005. "Work is going to be more giglike and short-term," Freelancers Union founder Sara Horowitz said. "This is a really big play, and there are lots of casts and plots and characters. Think about it—if I am a Web developer, I need to find copywriters, accountants, lawyers, and others." The Freelancers Union is an organization designed to support independent workers.

To access talent faster, creators match project needs with diverse minds anywhere. The December 2013 merger of oDesk and Elance, two Web sites aimed at connecting freelancers in short-term project-based work, built a combined company with eight million freelancers and approximately $750 million in combined yearly billings. Although that number seems enormous, it represents a mere 1.7 percent market share of the $422 billion global staffing market in 2013, as estimated by the Staffing Industry Analysts.

Freelancer.com connects nearly thirteen million users. Hourly-Nerd, a startup launched in 2013 by Harvard Business School students, seeks to pair MBA students with small businesses on project-specific needs. "HourlyNerd fills a need every entrepreneurial company faces," said serial entrepreneur Mark Cuban, an early investor in the startup. "I'm excited to be part of it and expect to use it heavily for all my portfolio companies." Thanks to technology-enabled global reach, flash teams increasingly define how work gets done.

Kirsten Saenz Tobey and Kristin Groos Richmond assemble flash teams to please one of the toughest customers on earth: the American child. In 2006, they launched Revolution Foods, aiming to deliver healthful school lunches to a few hundred children in Oakland, California. The two women saw poor-quality meals as one of the biggest problems in U.S. schools, particularly in low-income neighborhoods. Their solution: "Use the power of business to solve a social need," Tobey said. Today, Revolution Foods provides more than one million meals every week to students in more than a thousand schools.

"But you can't just show up with healthy options and expect kids to adopt it straightaway," Tobey explained. It took more than a thousand tries—for example, to create a chicken wing that wasn't deep-fried yet still won over young taste buds. Tobey and Richmond get daily reports on what is and is not working. A recent offering of cauliflower florets was rejected, but butternut squash was a surprising hit. "We have a couple hundred thousand kids that are eating our meals every day, and so a lot of it is continuous learning," Tobey said.

It's not just the kids who pose a challenge. Meals must meet the nutritional standards of the National School Lunch Program and cost less than $3 per unit to qualify for federal support. "With everything we design, we have to think about kid friendliness, operational feasibility, nutrition, price point, and compliance," Richmond said. To do this, they pull together diverse experts to create meal-by-meal menu solutions.

To make a healthful, tasty meatball, for example, Revolution Foods assembled a flash team of local suppliers, chefs, food production operators, dieticians, business planning people, local school administrators, and national supply-chain partners to find nutritious ingredients and the right way of cooking them. Traditional meatballs made from pork and beef can be high in fat and salt. To design a better dish, dieticians asked chefs, "Have you tried using this instead of that in the recipe?" Local producers discussed pricing, while supply-chain people addressed quantities to determine whether producing a million meatballs a month would be affordable.

"We think collectively about how we can get more nutrient-dense food that kids will like without adding a lot of sugar and salt and fat and oil," Tobey told me. "Most of the meat in the meatball is actually turkey, which is a very lean meat, but the flavor and spice taste more like a traditional meatball."

Proof that it worked came from students in the lunch line. The flash team's meatball became part of a spaghetti-and-meatballs meal and a meatball sandwich. Another Revolution Foods flash team performed an even greater miracle: creating an inexpensive yet nutritious hot dog that has satisfied young palates.

Because Tobey and Richmond use as much locally sourced, in-season produce as possible, developing new menu items is a constant project and flash teams are almost a necessity—which explains why the company maintains seven culinary centers across the country, close to local markets. "Conventional wisdom says that if you buy packaged goods, you save money," Richmond said. "But by buying raw ingredients and putting in the work, we're able to save a lot of money."

How do you feed hundreds of thousands of kids without deep frying or using packaged foods? Two moms making school lunches for a living found their answer by forming flash teams. Many prominent people, from First Lady Michelle Obama to celebrity chef Jamie Oliver, are addressing the problem of childhood obesity, and the founders of a for-profit business are at the forefront of the effort.

Pulling together diverse talent to achieve specific goals requires that individuals work quickly and productively together. Creators don't haphazardly assemble flash teams. They pay attention to team dynamics, often working with a mix of veterans and newcomers at the same time.

Brian Uzzi, a sociologist at Northwestern University, has studied creativity and collaboration extensively to better understand how relationships across networks influence success. "What we've found is that the biggest payback is when you have a core of a couple repeated relationships over multiple projects, with newcomer relationships coming and going over time across the different teams," Uzzi said.

If team members have little experience working together, they can struggle to communicate. Collaborating repeatedly with people you've known a long time speeds communication based on shared trust and an understanding of how they approach problems. But if team members are too familiar with one another, original ideas tend to be stifled. Newcomers bring fresh concepts and skills. The optimum is a mix: Teams operate best with both old and new members.

"When Rodgers and Hammerstein did musicals," Uzzi said, "they kept changing the other people who were part of their teams. The famous duo understood each other's approach and were able to communicate efficiently with each other, but they also needed newcomers to bring in fresh ideas to provoke creativity and innovation." Uzzi has examined team composition of 2,258 Broadway musicals from 1877 to 1990. Usually, six freelance artists assemble to create a musical: a composer, a lyricist, a librettist, a choreographer, a director, and a producer. The modus operandi may differ: *A Chorus Line* began with choreographer Michael Bennett creating a medley of dance numbers before Marvin Hamlisch added the music and others joined in, whereas *The Producers* began with librettist Mel Brooks's book. Projects originate from different vantage points, but the most successful teams are made up of a few trusted collaborators working alongside fresh talent through days of brainstorming, creative problem solving, editing, and intense exchange. Uzzi's research shows that this mix of veterans and newcomers is critical not only in the arts and entertainment but also in social psychology, economics, ecology, and astronomy.

If flash teams network minds by tapping into an individual's desire to work on specific problems and tasks, then prize competitions attract people based on the thrill of victory and the heady allure of winning something.

CATALYZE PRIZE COMPETITIONS

How do you pull a needle from a haystack? You just need the right hook. Prizes often provide an incentive that draws minds to solve challenges.

Prize competitions are not new. Charles Lindbergh won the $25,000 Orteig Prize for making the first nonstop flight from New

York to Paris. Inventors seeking prizes created fire extinguishers, canned goods, margarine, and other products. What is new, however, is the power of the Internet and mobile technology to bring people together.

Alpheus Bingham, for example, built InnoCentive, an online company centered on awarding prizes to those who could make scientific discoveries. Eli Lilly, Life Technologies, Roche USA, *Popular Science* magazine, and other prize sponsors use InnoCentive to engage more than 250,000 solvers—research scientists, academic faculty, physicians, technicians, and partners of all kinds. Approximately 60 percent of solvers have a master's degree or PhD. More than 40 percent come from Brazil, Russia, India, and China; 30 percent come from the United States, and the rest from more than 150 other countries.

Bingham believes in what he calls "the diverse exploration of space"—approaching science by broadcasting a problem to many people and comparing and evaluating the variety of ideas that result. An organic chemist, he learned in graduate school that many people tackling the same problem can devise original solutions. Bingham recalled being asked to solve a complex chemistry problem in a particular graduate course. Under pressure, he drew on what he knew, constructing a childhood chemistry set from his mother's cupboard. "No one else was thinking about cream of tartar," he said. "But I solved the problem." His class of twenty-five students produced twenty-five other solutions.

As a research scientist at Eli Lilly in 2001, Bingham observed that researchers were working in isolation, firm by firm, toiling separately to develop an AIDS vaccine. Bingham felt that scientists needed to build on each other's ideas. He brought Eli Lilly's top management an experiment he dubbed molecule.com. This online venture used the Web as a vehicle to outsource problem solving among the community of scientists. In 2005, the venture spun out of Eli Lilly to become InnoCentive.

"In the old days, you broadcast a prize in a very limited fashion. It was one direction, time dependent, and had limited reach," Bingham said. "You could put it in the *New York Times* and get *New York Times* readers that happened to turn to page fourteen on May 27." The Internet changed that. Bingham saw the Web as a tool for scientists to broadcast their problems and reach millions in the hope that a few could contribute pertinent knowledge. "Challenge Driven Innovation" is how Bingham describes networking minds through prize competitions.

In 2007, for instance, John Davis, an InnoCentive solver from the United States, won $20,000 from the Oil Spill Recovery Institute for his fix to clean up residual oil from the 1989 Exxon Valdez disaster off the Alaska coast. The institute posted the problem on Inno-Centive. Davis, a chemist, had no background in the oil industry. But he did know about a common construction method that uses vibrations to keep cement in liquid form longer to enable better pouring. Davis realized that the same approach would keep oil from freezing, allowing it to be pumped from recovery barges.

Seeking to develop a solar light that would function as a lamp and flashlight in the developing world, SunNight Solar reached out to the InnoCentive community. Within two months, an electrical engineer from New Zealand, Russell McMahon, solved the challenge to win $20,000.

The nonprofit TB Alliance posted a challenge to simplify the manufacturing process of a drug compound to improve its efficacy and lower the cost of treating tuberculosis, a disease responsible for one death every twenty seconds. Kana Sureshan was one of the winners of the TB Alliance Challenge, submitting a medicinal chemistry solution that will, in turn, benefit millions.

Questions range from how to make kitty litter odorless ($7,500 prize) to how to predict the progression of osteoarthritis ($10,000 prize). Scientists and others apply their knowledge to crack problems often outside their fields.

"Interestingly, the further the problem was from the solvers' expertise, the more likely they were to solve it," said Karim Lakhani, a Harvard Business School professor. Lakhani studied 166 InnoCentive challenges and concluded that if the problem fell outside a solver's expertise, the chance of success rose by 10 percent.

"The best solution does not always come from a Nobel laureate at Harvard," Bingham said. "It just might turn out that some kid in Romania has got a better idea worth pursuing." Prize competitions reach more than the usual suspects. Solutions often come from those new to a field because they can look at problems without the biases of industry standards.

Bingham uses the story of Archimedes to emphasize the importance of networking minds. In ancient Greece, King Hiero II needed to determine the gold content of a crown. As Archimedes entered a public bath, the story goes, he realized that displacement caused by lowering his body into the water was a principle that could be used to solve the king's problem. "Eureka!" he shouted. Bingham uses prize competitions "to get thousands of minds together in the hope that someone does take that all-crucial bath."

The value of prize competitions extends beyond one-time problem solving: Solutions often form the basis of business itself. Jake Nickell and Jacob DeHart, founders of Threadless, an online artists' community and e-commerce phenomenon, turned a T-shirt design competition into a business about the same time Bingham kicked off InnoCentive. In 2000, Nickell won a T-shirt design competition, and the adrenaline rush that accompanied it inspired him to something greater.

The thirty-three-year-old Nickell looks like an overgrown kid: shaggy hair, scruffy red beard, jeans, bright socks, tennis shoes, and a T-shirt hanging from his lean frame. He doesn't have an MBA—he never attended college—yet he has networked minds to make traditional retail look stodgy. His drawing card? Prize competitions. His mission? To raise the profile of artists and sell their designs worldwide.

When he won the T-shirt contest, Nickell was living in a tiny Chicago apartment while attending the Illinois Institute of Art at night and working at CompUSA, a computer retailer, during the day. In his spare time, he tapped into the online community Dreamless .org, a site hosted by Joshua Davis that attracted graphic designers, Web designers, and programmers. "It was a worldwide design misfit on the Internet," Nickell said: "people using code to create art and do weird things with their computers." Dreamless artists were the industry's finest at using Adobe Photoshop, Illustrator, Flash, and other design products. Nickell spent hours playing "Photoshop tennis" with friends from Dreamless, batting digital images back and forth and making photos ever more fantastic.

At the New Media Underground Festival, an informal gathering in London attended by many Dreamless members, organizers posted a T-shirt design contest. "I entered a design and I won!" Nickell exclaimed. "I was really excited that my design was being used." The T-shirt wasn't printed, and Nickell earned no money. His win meant little in practical terms. But it got him thinking.

The digital art Dreamless illustrators uploaded every day didn't go beyond the online realm. "I thought it would be fun to do real-world things, given all the time we spent making designs," Nickell told me. What if artists shared designs and voted on each other's work? He could print the best designs on T-shirts. Would they sell? Would this be a good way to give startup designers exposure? He posed the question to the Dreamless community. "That's how I started Threadless," Nickell said. He put up $500 to get started, and Jacob DeHart, a student at Purdue University and a friend from Dreamless, matched Nickell's investment.

The first competition received nearly 100 submissions; five were selected. The winners received two free shirts; any future proceeds from T-shirt sales would be reinvested in new contests. Artists began spending an average of six hours putting together their designs. They offered feedback on the designs of other illustrators. Soon, Threadless became a social network where designers exchanged ideas and critiqued each other's creations before voting on favorites. As artists solicited feedback and labored to improve their designs, they reached out to friends to vote for their submissions.

"Artists get feedback, and it motivates them to try even harder," Nickell explained. "It's almost like a drug where you have to keep getting better and better so people will respect and appreciate your work." The tight-knit community votes on designs, guaranteeing that the selected products have a ready-made market. In January 2001, when Nickell printed the first two dozen copies of Threadless's first five winning shirts, the designs sold out. "I really didn't know how to press T-shirts, charge cards, ship orders, or any of that," he admitted. But with a built-in audience, the business took off. In the beginning, he paid $50 to winners; the prize grew to $100, $250, and then $500. Today, winners receive $2,000 with a $500 gift certificate and royalties, not to mention the visibility that comes with the Threadless community.

"We print about 1 percent of the designs that come in," Nickell said. "We get 200 every single day." Up to ten designs are printed on T-shirts and distributed weekly online and at the Threadless retail store in Chicago, as well as through a partnership with The Gap.

Several extraordinary artists have been discovered through Threadless competitions. One winner became art director of Barack Obama's 2008 presidential campaign, another designed a line of snowboards for Burton, and another, Olly Moss, launched a successful career as a commercial artist after winning more than thirty Threadless contests.

This prize competition appeals far beyond the Threadless community. The company has hosted similar competitions to supply artwork for the cases of Dell laptops and Apple iPhones and iPads. In recent years, Threadless has expanded to create designs for water bottles, pillows, shower curtains, and wastebaskets for Bed Bath & Beyond, as well as creative content for Disney, the Cartoon Network, *Sesame Street*, and others.

Not surprisingly, the Threadless model is a success. As of 2014, the platform is almost two and a half million strong. More than 50 percent of the site's traffic comes from outside the United States. By using prize competitions, Nickell and DeHart have not only raised the profile of artists, but also built a thriving business.

GAMIFY WORK

From creating a commons and building flash teams to running contests, the unifying theme is that meaningful challenges can bring diverse minds together. Creators also use the power of games to pool brainpower and solve business issues. Games provide built-in metrics, timed performance, and immediate feedback.

Jane McGonigal, director of gaming for the Institute for the Future, argues that playing games with others improves relationships. The experience builds trust, creates a better understanding of others' strengths and weaknesses, and helps one know how to collaborate better in the future. Within gaming circles, individuals work together on common ground. Whether players win or lose, they build trust and cooperation. Games teach us to work together productively.

"We're hopefully going to change the way science is done by tapping the collective intelligence of people all over the world," said Zoran Popović, director of the Center for Game Science at the University of Washington in Seattle. In 2008, Popović and biochemist David Baker, also a professor at the University of Washington, released the game Foldit in an effort to engage thousands of players in the difficult but crucial task of folding proteins.

The human body has more than 100,000 different kinds of proteins, forming every cell and affecting the speed of every chemical reaction. Yet we don't know how proteins fold into complex shapes, given the endless possibilities for sequencing the amino acids that form proteins. "What's unknown is the geometric structure of many proteins," Popović said. "If you know the shape of any protein, you know the secret to life." It is a task that has defied computer analysis. Human intuition is essential to making progress. The game capitalizes on people's 3-D spatial ability to manipulate amino acid chains.

Many Foldit players describe the game as a twenty-first-century version of Tetris, a tile-matching video game. In the first several levels, players learn what good proteins look like and how to rotate them in three dimensions. They learn to pull the proteins' side chains together, bend overall protein backbones, and generate hydrogen bonds to maintain a stabilizing influence. Players manipulate multicolored geometric snakes that model protein configurations on a computer screen. It is beneficial to pack proteins tightly, but not too tightly. If they are too close, electrical charges in different side chains repel each other and spiky red burrs appear on the player's screen.

Players accumulate points based on how little energy it takes to fold their protein sequences into place. The best scores are made by players who can create the lowest-energy protein configurations.

Foldit promotes multiplayer competition by allowing people to team up, talk with each other, and develop group strategies. To intensify competition, Foldit gamers face off against research groups around the world in a major protein-structure competition every two years.

By harnessing the intelligence of more than 240,000 registered Foldit players, researchers improve the chances of finding treatments for cancer, Alzheimer's, and other diseases. To date, Foldit gamers have discovered small protein inhibitors to bind and block the virus that caused the global influenza pandemic of 1918. In 2011, Foldit gamers took just ten days to accomplish what biochemists had been trying to do for more than a decade—decode the structure of a protein called retroviral protease that is the key to how HIV multiplies. Understanding how this protein forms will help scientists develop drugs to combat the disease.

By networking minds through gaming, Popović has designed a way to pool the brainpower of thousands to help solve some of biology's most complex problems. "There is never a single person who can solve these things," he said. "We're optimizing for the collective development of expertise and making it fun for a lot of people."

Using game mechanics to solve professional challenges not only delivers results, it also taps into a growing phenomenon. More than a half-billion people worldwide play online games at least an hour a day, including 183 million in the United States. Creators understand that games can be more than simple entertainment; they can serve as valuable business tools to make work more compelling, interactive, and productive. By the end of 2014, technology research company Gartner predicts that more than 70 percent of the top 2,000 global companies will have used at least one type of game application.

PHD, a pioneering media and planning group within Publicis

Omnicom Group, a multinational advertising conglomerate, is at the forefront of using game mechanics to network minds. To foster improved employee collaboration and problem solving, the firm has developed a touch-screen game called Source that every PHD employee can play. Instead of the quests and puzzles found in consumer games, Source is oriented toward PHD's media planning and buying functions. Whether the task is organizing a brief, conducting market research, or tweaking a media campaign, PHD's employees can pursue it through the Source system.

Mark Holden, PHD's worldwide strategy and planning director, said, "When people come to PHD every day, it's a game. Work becomes play. Planning becomes socialized." The more they work in Source, the more collaborative people become, and the more points, or "pings," they accumulate. The pings are tracked via a real-time global leaderboard. PHD employees compete against others to see who can be the most productive and collaborative. Employees—the players—view the system's activity and see how many pings coworkers have received that day and for what piece of work

How an employee performs in Source can affect career advancement. The system provides motivation and feedback on performance, benefiting the organization. Its success was a major factor in Unilever's decision to award PHD most of its global communications planning work, according to Holden. "It's almost like there is one mind, one unconscious mind, working that you can just tap into where you can get fresh thinking that didn't exist before," he said.

Games hold out the promise of encouraging individuals to interact more effectively to take on responsibilities they otherwise might not assume and to generate fresh ideas. But, "it's very hard to actually pull it off," Popović said. Games need to be carefully designed to orient users toward the right goals. That means that business objectives need to be clearly identified up front—not always an easy task—and that the game must be properly structured to achieve them. At the same time, it's important to put players' interests first. If employees are to give it much of their precious time, the game must be engaging, but it must also be useful. It must be more than a game. Reward points and badges alone aren't enough to do the trick. Leveraging game mechanics to make work fun, measurable, and productive requires thoughtful design.

T-SHAPED PEOPLE

A world in which networking minds is a key to success requires a different kind of worker. Today we need not only to learn how to build on each other's ideas, but also to seize opportunities to create entirely new ways of bringing diverse minds together to solve problems.

Stanford University president John Hennessy speaks of the need to educate T-shaped people, those with depth in a certain area as well as the breadth and curiosity to speak the language of other disciplines. I-shaped experts have expertise in one field, whereas T-shaped people may be analytically focused on one area but are open enough to integrate other points of view.

Hennessy explains that collaboration sometimes allows you to "hit a grand slam by tackling problems that can't be approached from just one direction." Polio is one example: "Think of all the great people who were working on clinical therapies. They kept improving portable iron lungs, but that wasn't the solution. The solution was a vaccine." By linking different ways of thinking, scientists approached the problem differently. That trend is accelerating today: "The bandwidth between students is 100 megabits per second," Hennessy said. "They are exchanging information and broadening their skills in a way that supports the vision of a T-shaped person." Value comes from integrating expertise from across different fields.

The global workforce, with dissimilar experiences and divergent approaches, can deliver synergies. People who think differently, have different skills, speak different languages, or use different approaches and are able to network minds can craft innovative solutions.

If great minds think alike, networked minds combine multiple perspectives to solve complicated problems. Do you pick the safe choice? Or do you tackle the difficult challenge? Networking minds gives you the confidence and ability to take on problems that matter.

Chapter 6

GIFT SMALL GOODS

It is one of the most beautiful compensations of this life
that no man can sincerely try to help another without
helping himself.

—Ralph Waldo Emerson

They come for his classes. They come for his career advice. They come
to invest in his companies and license his patents. Leaders from academia, science, and business come seeking ideas and inspiration.
Even the president of the United States calls to seek his counsel. Bob
Langer assists.

Robert Langer runs the world's largest academic biomedical engineering lab in Cambridge, Massachusetts. Out of Langer's lab at
MIT come nanoparticles that target cancerous tumors, smart pills,

needleless injections, transdermal nicotine patches, regenerative human tissue, and even synthetic vocal cords that might one day help *Sound of Music* star Julie Andrews and others sing again. He's the man who grew a human ear on the back of a mouse. "The public relations wasn't great, but the science, that was fine," he said. Slight and unassuming, Langer has a humility that belies his stature as one of the world's most influential scientists.

Langer was the youngest person elected to all three American Science Academies. Credited with pioneering the fields of controlled-release drug delivery and human tissue engineering, he has cofounded twenty-five companies, licensed technology to more than 270 others, won more than 200 awards, filed more than 800 patents, and published some 1,200 papers. Yet when he is asked what he is proudest of, his answer is immediate: "My students. They're almost like my own kids. I get so much satisfaction seeing them do well."

Langer knows how crucial support can be. His career had, in his words, "a rocky start." After earning his doctorate in chemical engineering from MIT in 1974, he turned down more than twenty lucrative jobs in the oil industry. He wanted to teach. He applied to forty high schools and was turned down forty times. Stymied, he changed direction and applied for jobs as a medical researcher. He wrote letter after letter. No one responded.

Then Judah Folkman, a cancer surgeon at Boston Children's Hospital, invited Langer for a meeting. Langer drove to Children's in his beat-up Plymouth, wearing his only suit. Folkman, who died in 2008, was known as a maverick who sought to fight cancer by choking off the blood supply to cancerous cells. He took a gamble on the young chemical engineer, telling Langer that despite the complexity of the problem, he believed Langer had a shot at coming up with a solution. Folkman hired him, making him the only engineer in the hospital.

Langer spent two years trying to turn Folkman's theory into reality. "The only thing I had going for me was that I hadn't read the literature on why this was impossible," Langer said. He failed again and again. Then he hit on a breakthrough: a novel porous polymer that could house molecules that attack tiny blood vessels and control the rate at which they were released. This made it possible to stunt the growth of blood vessels that feed cancerous cells, creating a whole new class of effective cancer fighters.

Langer's research was ahead of its time. At first chemists and biologists dismissed it. Langer submitted nine grant proposals; all were rejected. He fought for years to get his first patents approved. Senior faculty at MIT thought his work was unimportant and told him as much. Through it all, Folkman supported him. "He put me on the path to doing the things I do today," Langer said, sitting on a lab stool. "The more I can do things like him, I think that's a real good thing."

WHAT'S A SMALL GOOD?

For creators (except perhaps for some of the most famously demanding and unpleasant ones), success is as much about caring about customers, colleagues, and partners as it is about building a novel product. Creators view caring as a competitive advantage and strengthen ties by paying attention to others' needs.

To build positive relationships, they look for ways to provide help—what I call gifting small goods. Creators are attentive to little gestures that might benefit others and reach out to offer assistance. The extra time and energy spent to forward a résumé, critique a proposal, give a reference, or write a few lines of code demonstrates that the creator cares about others and is willing to pitch in.

As the workplace shifts from the fixed work protocols of the automobile assembly line to more fluid environments, such as those used by people creating online products and services, professionals work from project to project, forming alliances that are crucial to pulling resources together quickly to accomplish goals. Factory workers at the end of an assembly line cannot influence decisions of the workers at its beginning. But in a less hierarchical work environment, professionals can choose whom to work with and influence outcomes by building mutually beneficial relationships.

Building new ideas requires energetic assistance from cofounders, investors, colleagues, advisers, and others. Creators need people who will help obtain information, test new ideas, identify partners, and quickly pull resources together. By thinking about ways to benefit others, creators develop allies willing to reciprocate. Paying attention to others' needs enlarges a creator's competitive edge.

The exchange of small favors also enhances one's professional reputation. Just a few years ago, it was difficult for outsiders to know how a boss treated her team. With online social networks, we can reference-check people quickly and easily. Transparency makes actions known. An individual's reputation for being particularly generous or particularly selfish can open or close doors. By fostering meaningful partnerships, creators become known as people others want to work with. This translates beyond individual person-to-person exchanges as trust is inferred across networks of colleagues. A positive reputation, spread by word of mouth, significantly enhances future opportunities.

Helping others has always been the right thing to do, but in today's transparent and connected world, it also makes creators more productive.

- "We're now at a point in history where it's in your self-interest to be good," Benchmark venture capital investor Matt Cohler told me. "And that's because the world is more transparent, interconnected, interdependent, and efficient." Cohler worked in the earliest teams at both LinkedIn and Facebook building a lot of today's transparency before becoming an investor.

- "In an age of transparency, honesty and generosity, even in the form of an apology, generate goodwill," said Alexander Asseily. "People think that you've behaved in a way that they would want an individual person to behave, and that experience makes them trust a brand and want to come back." It was a lesson the Jawbone cofounder learned after the company offered initial customers the option to get their money back and keep the UP bracelet when it malfunctioned.
- "We believe you do as well as those around you want to see you do," said Gilt Groupe's Alexis Maybank. By crafting mutually beneficial partnerships by giving of their time and energies, creators become known as people others want to work with.

Gifting small goods enables creators to create more value than they ever could alone.

A GIFT FOR GIFTS

"When people feel good about themselves, they solve problems," Bob Langer said as we walked between lab stations. "People can be insecure. I was. My job is to help encourage scientific confidence." Langer returns e-mails within minutes, reviews papers within twenty-four hours, and has an open-door policy for his students, from undergraduates to postdocs. He helps them get into graduate schools and find jobs, assists faculty with intellectual property agreements, offers venture capitalists insight on cutting-edge science, and gives policy-makers advice on how to bolster scientific research.

"Anytime you try to solve a problem to make a big impact, there's going to be a lot of challenges," Langer told me. "It's tough to go against prevailing wisdom." This makes collaborative help more essential.

Creators understand that pioneering new frontiers requires interde-pendent efforts. They find ways to work with, for, and through others to achieve results.

"I started to realize after doing research in my lab for a while, that you can only take it so far," Langer said. "If I wanted to do it to the point where you can really help people, you couldn't just do it in a lab at MIT; you need real industry to manufacture these systems."

Langer licensed his first polymer patents to Eli Lilly in the mid-1980s in exchange for research funding and a consulting fee. But the big pharmaceutical company let the technology languish. Dismayed, Langer fought to regain the rights to his patents, and with MIT col-league Alex Klibanov, he founded Enzytech, his first startup (which became Alkermes). It was risky to reject Lilly's funding; his actions reveal strength of character under his affable demeanor. Today, Al-kermes makes microspheres that deliver drugs to treat diabetes, schizophrenia, alcoholism, and other chronic diseases.

About the same time, a small company called Nova Pharmaceu-ticals approached Langer about licensing technology. He suggested a collaboration with Johns Hopkins neurosurgeon Henry Brem, renowned for his skill in removing brain tumors. The partnership led to the creation of the Gliadel Wafer, a polymer disc that delivers chemotherapy directly to the spot where a tumor has been removed from the brain. Previous cancer treatments would overwhelm a patient's body; this dime-size wafer can release drugs directly to a tumor site, sparing other tissue. The Gliadel Wafer was a breakthrough in cancer research and spurred the creation of a $12 billion company, with Langer on the board of directors. The experience convinced him that sharing scientific know-how with startups could create real impact.

"Since then, we have taken a lot of discoveries from my students in the lab and have made them into real products," Langer said. In fact, he has cofounded twenty-five companies that have exceeded $100 million in annual revenue each.

"He's spawned some very brilliant careers," said former postdoctoral student Marsha Moses, now director of the Vascular Biology Program at Boston Children's Hospital. More than 250 of Langer's former students have helped start companies or run divisions of larger pharmaceutical companies, and some 200 run labs of their own.

David Edwards is one of those former students. In the early 1990s, Edwards worked as the only mathematician in Langer's lab, modeling complex scenarios using math equations. Langer asked him whether he had considered modeling inhalable drugs, such as asthma therapies. Delivering less than 5 percent of the medicine into the lungs, inhalers are a poor mechanism for treatment. Edwards used his math skills to model how aerosol particles could be kept light, avoiding some of the pitfalls of standard treatments, such as the tendency of particles to stick to the back of the throat. His research led to successful lab studies, a publication, and the cofounding of Advanced Inhalation Research, or AIR, a company that was later sold for $114 million. (Langer helped here, too.) Edwards then became a professor of biomedical engineering at Harvard.

"The ideas can come from Bob or anyone else," postdoctoral student Pedro Valencia said as we walked past storage rooms marked with biohazard symbols and a team working on targeted nanoparticles, smaller than the diameter of a human hair. "Bob doesn't worry about who gets the credit. We focus on creating materials to relieve human suffering." In collaboration with Joseph Vacanti at Harvard's Massachusetts General Hospital, for example, Langer has used polymer scaffolds to create new skin for burn victims and new cartilage for spinal cord repair. Recently, Langer Lab researchers snipped the spinal cords of rats, grew replacement cells on polymer scaffolding, and implanted them where the cord had been severed. The rodents walked again, although with a limp. This breakthrough could one day help paralyzed people walk again. "This work could be the dawn of someday making all kinds of new tissues: spinal cords, intestines, livers, tracheas," Langer said.

Inventing new solutions invariably requires battling convention. Creators gift small goods to build meaningful partnerships. They find allies where they can and commit themselves to championing others.

"The question at the end of the day is, 'How many therapies and products will have Bob's fingerprints on them?'" said Boston University president Robert Brown. "I think the number will be huge, and the quality of people's lives will be greatly improved because of them."

COOPERATION IS CONTAGIOUS

Gifting small goods can be contagious. Phillip Kunz, a sociologist at Brigham Young University, conducted a fascinating experiment in the science of generosity. He randomly selected 600 people from all socioeconomic classes and sent them Christmas cards. He signed them "Merry Christmas from Phil" in red pen.

Kunz received 117 cards in return. Many were rather generic, signed with nothing more than "Merry Christmas." Some stated the obvious: "For some reason we failed to recall that we know you, when you sent your Xmas card. Happy Holidays to you anyway." Others included photographs of new houses, babies, or pets, along with detailed letters that "recalled their old friendship." In addition, Kunz received eleven calls from people either curious to discover who he was or looking to catch up with someone they presumed was a long-forgotten friend.

The experiment revealed that many people try to repay small kindnesses. We've all had random exchanges in daily life that we reciprocate: a sympathetic smile, the holding of a door, a compliment from a stranger. Generosity can set off a chain reaction.

In December 2012, a drive-through customer of a Tim Horton's coffee shop in Winnipeg, Manitoba, paid for the order of the stranger in the car behind her in line. Her act sparked a ripple effect: The next 226 customers who ordered at the drive-through paid for the following person. In 2013, a Chick-fil-A in Houston reported a sixty-seven-car chain of customers who paid for the next person. A few months later, a Heav'nly Donuts in Amesbury, Massachusetts, took note of a fifty-five-car chain.

Exchanges of generosity create a multiplier effect of three to five times the magnitude of the initial contribution. Professors James Fowler of the University of California at San Diego and Nicholas Christakis of Yale University call this phenomenon "social contagion." Recipients of generosity are more likely to be generous in future exchanges. "When people benefit from cooperation, they don't go back to being their old selfish selves," Fowler explained.

In a 2010 study, Fowler and Christakis found that generosity begets generosity and sparks collaboration. In the experiment, four strangers came together to play a game. "It's like a big Sudoku or round robin," Fowler said. Each person received twenty cents and was asked to decide, in secret, what to keep and what to contribute to a common fund, to be split equally. The best payoff would come if all four players put all their money into the kitty; however, without knowing what other participants were going to do, each had to make a choice. Only afterward would the players learn the collective result. The game was then repeated, with each player assigned to a different group of four.

"What you see is that a single act of cooperation in round one influences the behavior of someone for the rest of the game," Fowler explained. Every dollar given in the first round caused recipients to give an extra twenty cents in the second round; people who played with these participants gave an extra eight cents in the third round; those who played in the fourth round gave an extra five cents. "This doesn't necessarily sound like a lot of money, all of these nickels and dimes," Fowler said, "but when you add it up, each extra dollar of giving caused a cascading effect like a matching grant contributing an extra three dollars."

This research highlights how acts of generosity can create significant gains. In more fluid modern work environments, individuals can influence and benefit from the cooperation engendered by gifting small goods.

CASE IN POINT: LINKEDIN'S REID HOFFMAN

"It's people first," LinkedIn cofounder Reid Hoffman said when we met at a Palo Alto café. "It's the people around you that make you an effective professional—getting information, accomplishing tasks, making transactions happen, and getting opportunity flow for you and the people who matter to you." Hoffman excels in the networked economy. In fact, he had a hand in creating it.

Ellen Levy, a mutual friend, said, "Reid is the kind of guy who would mow your lawn if you needed help." Levy worked for LinkedIn after founding management consultancy Silicon Valley Connect. Her comment underscores how gifting small goods can become an everyday activity. What is new is the online connectivity that makes these actions visible.

"It's not as if others will lie across railroad tracks for you, but they will think about how things could be useful for you," Hoffman said. "If you've focused on little things that you can do that are beneficial to others, most people will care about you and be eager to help." That's one of the reasons that entrepreneurs, investors, and policymakers reach out to Hoffman: He tries to help. Even if he declines to invest in a company after hearing an entrepreneur's pitch, he still tries to lend a hand. "I like to give advice and be helpful," he said. Gifting small goods has earned Hoffman a reputation as a go-to investor in Silicon Valley.

Although Hoffman helps others, make no mistake: His actions are collaborative, not altruistic. "What's cool about a lot of business work is that it's a non–zero-sum game," Hoffman said. "People are out there making sure to do small things for one another. Online tools facilitate this, and subsequently, a massive amount of value is created. Most people misunderstand networking because most of the people who describe themselves as networkers take." Hoffman shook his head. "By focusing on how you can help others around you, that has a mammoth benefit for you."

The rationale for LinkedIn is based on game theory. "Game theory works when you create a system that is multi-transactional and the people are transacting continually," Hoffman explained. "Others can't burn you because it always comes back to them." Hoffman structured LinkedIn so that it's easy to assess other people's reputations. Members of LinkedIn connect with colleagues and classmates, who in turn can make introductions to potential employers, employees, clients, or customers. In a sense, the online professional network creates an economic incentive for everyone to behave better. "You have to realize that it is a small world in which people can track you down," Hoffman said.

Hoffman started as a Stanford philosophy major and studied as a Marshall Scholar at Oxford. He describes himself as a public intellectual, and though he considered a career in academia, he decided he "could create software that has the same kind of impact that public intellectual activity does but with the power of the commercial model behind it, which means that it can scale to reach millions, if not tens of millions of people." Driven by building consumer technology businesses that scale, he focuses on building mutually beneficial relationships.

"People used to think that you're happy to be following me because I'm a 'big person,'" Hoffman said, "but now it's more about focusing on the health of the people who are following you." He noted the changing patterns of leadership. Given the competitive nature of today's world, people at all levels and stages of their careers need to attract allies as employees, investors, or mentors. How? "It's helpful to have a bunch of money from which to pay them," Hoffman said. "But high-quality people can be well paid by a number of people, so your project has to be interesting and you have to be interesting." Creators attract others by providing them opportunities and finding ways to promote their careers.

That is evident in the way Hoffman operates. In the earliest days of YouTube, he gave YouTube founders Jawed Karim, Chad Hurley, and Steve Chen free office space at LinkedIn. As an angel investor, he has supported the founders of Flickr, Groupon, Mozilla, Digg, Mightybell, Technorati, and Tiny Pictures. Hoffman is the person who introduced Mark Zuckerberg to his college friend Peter Thiel, after which Thiel made the first outside investment in Facebook. Hoffman contributes as a board member to Airbnb, Edmodo, Xapo,

Mozilla Corporation, Wrapp, and Shopkick, and nonprofits Endeavor, Questbridge, and Kiva.org. In 2012, to accelerate Kiva's microlending activity, he lent $1 million of his money as an incentive to draw 40,000 new members, giving $25 microloans to entrepreneurs in the developing world. Kiva received two months' worth of traffic in a matter of days.

To describe how collaboration and competition work together, Hoffman draws a parallel to his favorite board game, Settlers of Catan. The first person to have ten victory points wins, but the only way to win is by trading with others. "You can't build without borrowing," Hoffman explained. "You're all competing, but you must trade in order to advance. You must establish relationships and figure out why people are or aren't trading with you. We joke about using this for recruiting to see how people play and think." Each player attempts to build an empire by capturing spaces on the board. To do so, players can trade resources, make alliances, conspire, strategize, lend a hand, or punish others. Many in Silicon Valley agree that playing Settlers resembles shaping entrepreneurial strategy, as players swap resources and are forced to revamp plays by rolls of the dice. Being an avid Settlers fan dovetails with Hoffman's practice of gifting small goods.

GIFT GUIDE

Creators use certain principles to gift goods effectively. They decide whom they will help, establish parameters for the time and effort they will invest, and interact with others through repeated exchanges.

DECIDE WHOM TO HELP

Referrals from trusted colleagues are nearly universally required. Reid Hoffman explained: "The only times that I work with people are when someone comes strongly recommended to me through a source that I trust." LinkedIn is set up on the same principle. Sara Blakely's filter is women as first-time entrepreneurs. She strives to give women a leg up by featuring their fledgling businesses on the Spanx Web site and in Spanx catalogs. Threadless cofounder Jake Nickell looks for ways to promote unknown artists. "One girl, who got her design printed for Gap, is a stay-at-home mom with two really young kids living on an Army base and her husband was just sent off to Iraq," Nickell said. "After she put her kids to sleep at night, she worked on her design." Creators support those who share their values.

SET PARAMETERS FOR TIME AND EFFORT

Bob Langer manages his tight schedule by parceling out advice and contacts in fifteen- and thirty-minute appointments. He makes himself available and responds to requests in real time, but he keeps the conversations efficient. For Joe Lonsdale, cofounder of Palantir, Addepar, and Formation 8, the standard entails the nature of the problem to be solved: "Unfortunately, many technology companies are about self-expression, having fun, and teaching a pet to tweet. I'm interested in helping my friends confront problems important for civilization around energy, health care, government, and finance." Gifting small goods deepens relationships and broadens connections, but creators stay productive in pursuit of their own work.

BE INTERACTIVE

Hamdi Ulukaya, the founder of Chobani, hired former Kraft employees after purchasing a dilapidated dairy plant. He built partnerships with upstate New York dairy farmers who had fallen on hard times. When Chobani needed help in its factory, a good working relationship with the local community fueled Chobani's growth. As business school students, Alexis Maybank and Alexandra Wilkis Wilson completed a research project for Susan Posen, then CEO of her son Zac Posen's design company. When they needed help starting Gilt Groupe, they asked for a favor—and their online fashion site was launched with Zac Posen as its first designer.

Stanford professor Frank Flynn conducted research on generosity and frequency of favor exchange by surveying 161 engineers in a Silicon Valley company and discovered that the most productive engineers often offered to help their colleagues. But he also found that some of the least productive engineers were equally generous. The difference came in *how* they gifted small goods. High achievers interacted constantly. Their ability to help colleagues earned them respect and social status, and their willingness to ask for favors helped them work more efficiently. The less productive engineers offered to help others but didn't ask for help in return. Their generosity drained their own resources and hindered their productivity. The key is to interact in an ongoing give-and-take of mutually beneficial assistance.

WEED'S COROLLARY TO MOORE'S LAW

"My joke is that I want what I never had in college: I want to be first on everyone's speed dial," said Jeff Weedman, one of the founding leaders of Procter & Gamble's Connect + Develop. Through Weedman's team, P&G—the world's largest consumer company, with $83 billion in annual revenue—seeks partnerships with companies, developers, innovators, and scientists to harness innovative ideas. Weedman helped create Connect + Develop, an open innovation platform, as an internal P&G startup.

"P&G hit a wall about ten years ago," Weedman said. "Our innovation had slowed. We were successful on only a third of our initiatives." P&G wanted to build a reputation for being a gracious partner and fair competitor. "It sounds like a soft goal, but it's real," Weedman told me. "We measure how we stack up against other corporate cultures, asking, 'Do people like to be partners with us?'" A shift toward focusing outward for P&G meant building alliances with other companies, including competitors.

A few years ago, a contact called Connect + Develop with a fascinating technology, but because it didn't align with P&G's businesses, Weedman referred the person to his counterpart at a direct competitor. At the next industry association meeting, the other company's innovation director thanked him for the lead. "My biggest problem was getting my team to look at it because you had referred it," she explained. "It took me a while to convince them that this was totally in keeping with how you operate: If it doesn't fit with P&G, you will pass it on."

"I want people to know that calling me first is always the thing to do," Weedman said. "If we're interested, we'll go ahead. If we're not interested, we won't block it. In fact, we'll help others move it forward." It's common sense for Weedman; gifting small goods generates value that outweighs any potential cost to P&G. "That's important currency," he explained.

"I have Weed's Corollary to Moore's Law"—the theory that computer chip performance doubles every eighteen months—Weedman said. "The second deal with the same company is half as long as the first, the third deal takes a third less time, and so on and so forth. Typically, the second deal and third deal are bigger in value and unidentifiable when the first deal is done." Of course, once issues such as intellectual property rights agreements and other legal issues are settled, future transactions likely move more quickly. But Weedman believes that "the trust factor" leads to exploring ways to find future benefit for both companies. Awareness of what partners can do opens doors. People begin to say, "Oh, I didn't know you could do that!" or "Oh, what if we did this?"

The Pampers Kandoo brand licensing agreement with Nehemiah Manufacturing demonstrates Weed's Corollary. P&G considered its Kandoo toddler's brand too small and a distraction from its other lines, so it offered it to a Cincinnati-based social enterprise and manufacturing company, Nehemiah Manufacturing. In return, Nehemiah cofounder Dan Meyer has referred business to P&G that was too large a partnership for Nehemiah to manage. Over the past few years, Nehemiah has licensed nine P&G brands. In 2012, Weedman introduced Meyer to Julie Pickens and Mindee Doney, founders of Little Busy Bodies, a brand of children's cleansing wipes.

What is Weedman gaining by introducing Dan Meyer to another industry partner? "I don't know," Weedman said. "It's helping a company we're doing business with, so that's good. And I will guarantee something good will happen, but I don't know what that is. There is an element that is data driven, but we do these things on faith."

THE SNUGGLE FOR EXISTENCE

"Cooperation is not just a small phenomenon," said Martin Nowak, director of the Program for Evolutionary Dynamics at Harvard University. "It is something that is really needed to explain the world as we see it." Nowak argues that Charles Darwin's theory of evolution needs an update. In addition to mutation and natural selection, evolution requires a third mechanism: cooperation.

Nowak asserts that the formation of language is the most interesting phenomenon of the past 600 million years, and that the ability to communicate enables a mode of evolution tied to ideas, not genetics alone.

I had heard about Nowak's "Mathematics of Evolution" and arrived at the Evolutionary Dynamics lab to find math equations scribbled across every wall. A friendly professor with an Arnold Schwarzenegger accent—Nowak grew up in the same part of Austria as the former governor and action movie hero—greeted me.

To unravel complex decision-making strategies that underpin human behavior, Nowak uses computer models and game theory to simulate exchanges between people. Perhaps the best-known example is the Prisoner's Dilemma. In this scenario, two criminal suspects are arrested, interrogated separately, and offered a deal. If one prisoner "defects" by incriminating the other, he will be freed, but his accomplice will be jailed for ten years. If both "cooperate" by remaining silent, each receives a one-year sentence. If both defect, each serves five years in jail. The rational choice is to defect and hope the other guy doesn't betray you.

In the Prisoner's Dilemma, the prisoners are separated. Had they been able to make a pact, they would have agreed not to incriminate each other and served just one year, but because they cannot communicate, each does what appears to be the rational thing and defects—and so both serve five-year terms. Communication changes everything.

Nowak and his colleagues developed a version of the Prisoner's Dilemma in which players acquire reputations. When reputations spread quickly, cooperation increases. Being selfish provides an advantage in the short term but not over the long run with repeated exchanges. Defectors are unable to fool other players as easily, and the advantage lessens.

"People gain reputations that precede them," Nowak said. This is increasingly true in today's world of instantaneous communication via mobile technology and social media. "You help because reputation matters and helpful people will be helped," Nowak said. "You also hear about others' reputations and help them according to whether they have helped in the past." Communication makes cooperation more fundamental.

"I help you and someone else helps me," Nowak explained. "I don't expect reciprocity necessarily from you, but based on reputation, where someone observes my behavior and spreads it through gossip, others observe my actions as well." Reputation has a powerful effect on interactions. People who have a reputation for not cooperating tend to be shunned while cooperative players get rewarded.

Nowak's research shows that in pursuing our self-interested goals, we have an incentive to act generously toward others. Given that others repay kindnesses with kindness, we further our own interests.

"Nice guys finish first," asserted David Rand, a former research scientist in Nowak's lab and today an assistant professor at Yale University. Rand took Nowak's mathematical model one step further to study repeated interactions among strangers in an online network. In 2011, he conducted an experiment with more than 800 participants drawn from Amazon's Mechanical Turk online marketplace. Each individual was connected to one or more players in a game in which everyone was given an equal number of points they could share—or not share—with connections. As expected, people benefited from cooperation. Others wanted to ally with those who had been helpful and sever ties with those who had not. In the real world, too, because people control whom they interact with, they are more likely to form connections with others who are cooperative and break ties with people who don't help.

Of particular interest to Rand were the reactions of players who had not originally acted cooperatively. Threatened by the loss of connection, these individuals were twice as likely to share their points with others the next time. Realizing the penalty for not cooperating—being shunned—these players overcompensated in succeeding rounds by being more cooperative than others.

"Basically, what it boils down to is that you'd better be a nice guy, or else you're going to get cut off," Rand said.

Researching and writing this book has been possible because creators generously gifted small goods. More than 200 creators offered their insights, gave hours of their time, answered myriad questions, and followed up via phone, e-mail, or Skype. Nearly every conversation ended with an offer: "Let me know how else I can help . . . I'll put you in touch with another entrepreneur you should interview . . . We're here if you need anything else." Their generosity is an inspiration, but it is also a skill. Creators are remarkable not just for the organizations they have built but for how they have built them.

Conclusion

THE POWER OF SIX

Whatever you can do, or dream you can do, begin it.
Boldness has genius, power, and magic in it.

—W. H. Murray

In the mid-1990s in Palo Alto, California, computer programmer Pierre Omidyar made a Sunbird leap. "I'm inspired by ideas and by taking ideas from one sector to another," Omidyar told me. Spotting the opportunity to bring person-to-person sales to the online world, he proposed a sort of Internet flea market to his friend Jeff Skoll. At the time, Skoll was managing online distribution channels for a subsidiary of the Knight Ridder newspaper chain. "I saw the gap that Pierre described," Skoll said. "I quit my job, and we went to work."

Omidyar's inspiration, eBay, grew quickly. He and Skoll moved fast to stay ahead of larger competitors that could quash their enterprise before it got out of the startup phase. But the same breakneck pace essential to survival became, Skoll said, "our Achilles' heel." The eBay Web site began to experience system breakdowns as traffic surged. The two kept their eyes on the horizon. "Entrepreneurs see past obstacles," Skoll declared. But in 1999, the site crashed for four days. "At one point, we looked at each other and said, 'What are we going to do? The company's dead!'" Skoll recalled, shaking his head. They pulled together enough brainpower from different technical fields to find a fix. Within five years, eBay went from being an idea in one man's head to a cultural icon with hundreds of millions of users. "The secret sauce was the belief that people are basically good," Omidyar explained. Just as they hoped, buyers and sellers built trust online, allowing eBay to host a volume of transactions that seemed to grow at lightning speed.

"I remember thinking we never studied cases like this at business school that required so many smarts all at once," Skoll told me. "We had companies that were trying to buy us; we were looking to raise venture capital; our technology was crashing; we were growing our staff exponentially. Everything happened simultaneously."

Omidyar and Skoll cracked the code. They brought together the six essential skills that allowed eBay to flourish. But they had to discover the code on their own. You have the blueprint.

APPLYING THE CODE

Creators tap six essential skills to start successful enterprises. Each skill is useful on its own, but remarkably, each one sustains the others. Just as putting together the dashes and dots of Morse code allows us to form words and ideas, combining the six skills unleashes tremendous possibilities.

The code seems obvious once it is revealed, but it is difficult to unlock without the key. One entrepreneur's experience doesn't reveal how creators break through. It took 200 interviews and untold hours of research to unlock the answer.

In the course of the book, we've examined stories of extraordinary entrepreneurs. Chipotle's Steve Ells, whom we met in Find the Gap, didn't just see an opportunity to create a fast-casual restaurant chain; he outmaneuvered the competition with a steadfast commitment to creating healthier fast food. Opower founders Dan Yates and Alex Laskey didn't just Fail Wisely to test ideas; they drew together academics, legislators, utility company managers, and software programmers to find a new way to conserve energy. All of the creators you've met in this book have mastered all six skills.

And the six skills aren't the monopoly of a special category of person. They aren't rare gifts or slim-chance talents. They are accessible to all of us. Each skill can be developed and cultivated. Once you know the code, you can apply it to your next endeavor.

When Skoll started Participant Media in 2004, he reapplied the skills he had learned at eBay. He identified a gap in Hollywood's film offerings—message-oriented movies such as *Schindler's List* were rare—and spent a year talking with actors, agents, lawyers, writers, directors, producers, and studio executives to explore the opportunity. "The surest way to become a millionaire is to start by being a billionaire and go into the movie business," he was told. (When eBay went public in 1998, Skoll owned 22 percent of the company, enough to make him a billionaire.) "Oftentimes, spotting an opportunity comes hand in hand with someone saying that something can't be done," Skoll said.

He launched Participant Media and quickly made some key decisions. One was a commitment to turn Al Gore's climate change presentation into a film. "I agreed to it on the spot," Skoll said. But for every *An Inconvenient Truth*, he has produced movies such as *Man from Plains* or *The Beaver* that have attracted little attention. "Of ten films, you expect five or six of them to fail, two or three to be wobbly and break even, and one to break out and cover the losses in the rest of the portfolio," Skoll explained. "Everything is a bet. A movie is a bet. An Internet short video is a bet. An investment is a bet. And the trick is making enough bets so that you can actually learn."

In Hollywood, Skoll assembles flash teams that work in short bursts to make and market films. Understanding that relationships matter, he takes risks to support others even when the odds are long. Actor George Clooney asked Skoll to read a script for a black-and-white film, written in four acts. All the other major studios had refused the project, a period piece about crusading broadcast journalism in the McCarthy era. Skoll backed it. "It wasn't very good, but George's passion sold me," he said. It turned out to be *Good Night and Good Luck*, a movie that earned six Academy Award nominations, including Best Picture.

By employing the six skills time and again, Skoll and his team at Participant Media have produced more than fifty movies, which have collectively received seven Academy Awards and thirty-six nominations. Five of his films have surpassed $100 million in earnings: *Charlie Wilson's War* ($119 million), *The Help* ($212 million), *Contagion* ($135 million), *The Best Exotic Marigold Hotel* ($137 million), and *Lincoln* ($275 million).

You may ask yourself what you have in common with creators such as Jeff Skoll. The answer: more than you think. They aren't superhuman. Skoll paid his way through college by pumping gas. Kevin Plank started Cupid's Valentine, an annual business that sold roses for Valentine's Day, to raise seed money for Under Armour. Threadless cofounder Jake Nickell dropped out of art school. From ordinary beginnings come extraordinary outcomes. No credentials are required. Curiosity and a willingness to work matter most.

But the code requires that we reframe how we think about the world. Schools prepare us to believe there is a single right answer. Standardized tests have taught us to think in a standardized way. But that's not how the world works, as much as we may want it to. A fundamental shift is occurring as business moves away from solving complicated but defined problems to seizing unique angles and bringing new ideas to life.

"It requires taking responsibility for your own learning," Dropbox cofounder Drew Houston explained. "Running a startup on any given day, you're sort of yo-yoing between euphoria and terror and just getting used to it." There's more to it than just an idea. It takes grit, daring, and the capacity to persuade others to join you in building a vision worth pursuing. "It takes looking crazy and not caring, and thinking it's fun and funny," Stella & Dot founder Jessica Herrin explained, then quipped, "There are no jobs on the unicorn farm." Simply put, no perfect job exists.

You can rely on the code to unlock future endeavors, even as the challenges entrepreneurs face keep changing. Every creation is singular. There are moments that reveal gaps to fill. Then they disappear, and fresh opportunities open. The next Steve Jobs may pioneer technology in the health-care field, as Elizabeth Holmes has done with lab testing. The Bill Gates of tomorrow may resemble Joe Lonsdale, one of those "weird computer scientists" obsessed with "solving hard problems with technology." There is no one way to create. And no two businesses will be the same.

It takes courage to bring something original into the world. "Creativity takes courage," the painter Henri Matisse famously said.

But creating companies is like painting on water, working with fluctuating market forces and ever-changing competitive threats.

BELIEVING IN YOURSELF, BELIEVING IN YOUR IDEA

The cornerstone of creators' success is their unshakable belief in their own abilities and powerful desire to bring change to the world. It takes optimism, figuring out what needs to be done, then taking action. The promise isn't that it will be easy, but that it will be worth it. Yelp started slowly before it became a business review site; it took Tesla Motors seven years to manufacture its first car; Revolution Foods has brought healthy meals to underprivileged students one school at a time. Every breakthrough has a backstory.

"You have to believe you can get to the other side," Jawbone cofounder Hosain Rahman told me, describing how he has met the challenge of making complicated hardware and software simple to use. "You have to believe that uniqueness matters," Peter Thiel said. "You need the conviction that you can build things and change things and improve people's lives," Max Levchin declared. "I grew up on the other side of the Iron Curtain, and to me the idea of entrepreneurship is this really romantic notion of capitalism."

Creation is at bottom an act of faith, a commitment to a dream of the future. All of us hold within ourselves the potential to become creators, and the expanding universe of entrepreneurship provides infinite pathways for us to explore—if we dare. Look at the world around you. It's a world that's perpetually changing, perpetually being made. Only you can seize the tremendous power that is yours and become one of the world's creators.

ACKNOWLEDGMENTS

A number of people believed in this book from the very start. I am grateful to each and every one.

To the more than two hundred entrepreneurs who generously shared their experiences, insights, and precious hours: You literally made this project possible. When I first set out to write a book, I didn't realize that it would take years of research before the first words appeared on my laptop screen. You taught me that the act of creation takes time, courage, passion, and resilience. When I began, I thought I would get back to my former life after a short writing sabbatical. I learned that you don't get back—you come out different. I'm deeply changed and profoundly inspired by the creators I interviewed and their way of work.

While I was still working in the White House, the brilliant author Tom Peters encouraged me to write and was a great help in crucial moments. He also introduced me to Donna Carpenter, who, together with Maurice Coyle, provided keen editorial judgment and insightful comments on drafts. Thanks also to Vince Ercolano, Sally Atwater, and Lisa Moscatiello for copyediting.

To my research team, thank you for your commitment, long hours, hard work, and, most of all, for making it fun. Alex Kapur, thank you for sifting through hundreds of academic studies and talking to me about them for years. Joanna Prusinska, I'm ever grateful to you for transcribing interviews, fielding research queries, and helping put the book over the finish line. Brian Gowen, you did yeoman work analyzing companies. Dana Abu-Nasrah, you are a social media maven. Cody Reneau, thank you for enrolling in NASCAR driving school with me to learn how to manage speed. (I'm still sure I lapped you on Road Atlanta.) Thanks as well to Robert Lynch, Alice Sweitzer, Sachin Anand, Julie Kraut, Morgan Hargrave, Todd Schweitzer, Zhizhou Zhu, Mohammad Modarres, Steven Hoffman, Chardet Durbin, and Lauren Kane.

Lee Hamilton brought me into the Woodrow Wilson International Center for Scholars as a public policy scholar and I am honored to continue my affiliation as a global fellow. Heartfelt thanks to Mike Van Dusen, Rob Litwak, Lucy Jilka, John Dysland, John Tyler, Lee's successor Jane Harman, and everyone else at the Center who supported my work. Special thanks to Janet Spikes and her crack team at the Wilson Center library for their unflagging assistance.

I have also been fortunate to be a senior fellow at the Harvard Kennedy School of Government in the Center for Business and Government and the Center for Public Leadership. It has been a privilege to collaborate with David Gergen, Richard Zeckhauser, John Haigh, Roger Porter, Jack Donahue, Scott Leland, Jennifer Nash, Max Bazerman, Patricia Bellinger, Owen Andrews, and Tom Novak.

The Ewing Marion Kauffman Foundation supported my research, for which I am deeply grateful. I would like to give particular thanks to Yasuyuki Motoyama, a senior scholar at the Kauffman Foundation, for his shared interest in high-scale entrepreneurs.

My thanks also to the Simon & Schuster team for your talent, patience, and enthusiasm. I feel a strong sense of gratitude to Jon Karp for believing in this book. I thank Ben Loehnen for his extraordinary ability, stewardship, and many excellent suggestions that made the book better. Brit Hvide offered valuable feedback and shepherded the book through production. My gratitude also goes to Emily Loose and Dominick Anfuso who backed the idea in its earliest days.

Kim Witherspoon and Michael Carlisle at Inkwell Management signed a first-time writer. Thank you for being in my corner. Eric Rayman helped navigate and advise at crucial moments. Thank you for your wise counsel.

I owe tremendous gratitude to Steve Lagerfeld, former editor of the *Wilson Quarterly*, who guided me through every step of the way. I don't have words for how much Steve helped me with words. He is an exceptional editor and even finer person.

One of my greatest blessings is to have smart, generously spirited friends like Annmarie Sasdi, Myrna Hymans, Joyce Said Ward, Lou O'Neil, Charles Cross, and Amy Gilliam, who have offered me their homes as writing retreats and stayed up late to hear about the latest interview for the book. I am ever grateful to my close friends and personal board of advisers: Jim and Olivia Jones, Kathleen Miller, Jamie Stiehm, Katie McNerney, Lisa Hayes, Carmen Suro-Bredie, Vanessa Moore, Chris Abraham, Porter Bibb, Paula Silver, Herbert Winokur, Marsh Carter, Juleanna Glover, John Bryson, Kristin Canavan, John Maull, Alissa Douglas, Anne Haack, Melissa Gallagher-Rogers, Melissa Paoloni, Beverly Kirk, Charles Holloway, Charles O'Reilly, Joel Peterson, Uta Kremer, Lenny Mendonca, Christopher Michel, George Kurian, Ben Kershberg, Laura Lovelace, Larry Altman, Andrew Rosen, Binta Brown, Drew Erdmann, Vijay Vaitheeswaran, Cait Murphy, David Wessel, and Rajiv Chandrasekaran.

Thanks also to my Stanford Business School classmates, who seemed always to be coming out of the woodwork to make introductions, read chapter drafts, help build my Web site, and invite me to give speeches. I'm grateful for what long-term partners do for each other. And right back at you!

Most of all, I am grateful to my parents, Judy and John Wilkinson. Thank you for creating a world in which anything was possible and for teaching me, by example, to work hard, champion others, and be an original. Your unwavering support has made this book and so many other dreams come true. To my brother, David Wilkinson, thank you for the love, extraordinary kindness, quirky encouragement, and purity of soul that makes being your sister such a gift. My grandmother Nadine Girod began to encourage me to write a book when I was about in fourth grade. As it got underway, my 97-year-old grandma and her 103-year-old boyfriend were the first to offer to host a book party. Nadine and Red, you inspire me. We'll launch *The Creator's Code* in Salem, Oregon. To my family and friends who count as family, this book could not have been written without your high fives, big hugs, long walks, belly laughs, tearful truths, occasional kicks in the pants, and never-ending words of encouragement.

To everyone who helped make this book a reality, thank you from the bottom of my heart. My hope is that the effort will help inspire others to unleash their own unique ability to create.

APPENDIX: RESEARCH METHODOLOGY

PROJECT DESCRIPTION

How are creators able to achieve the massive scaling of enterprises? What actions and processes do these individuals undertake to start and grow ventures to more than $100 million in annual revenue or 100,000 people served? The purpose of my research was to identify a set of core skills that creators develop to achieve high-scale results.

In this project, I was guided by two main research objectives: First, to identify a select group of creators who started and led new ventures to significant national and, in some cases, international levels; and second, to conduct exhaustive case studies of these individuals to determine the specific actions and skills that propel them to achieve such remarkable results.

To accomplish this, I devised a rigorous four-stage methodology to help assess with confidence that I had, in fact, identified and evaluated some of the most successful creators scaling high-growth ventures and shaping entrepreneurial ecosystems.

Research Phase 1: Evaluating Scholarly Research

Given the interdisciplinary nature of entrepreneurship and this project, I examined academic research across disciplines of entrepreneurship, organizational behavior, economics, psychology, sociology, creativity, decision theory, and strategy to do a literature review. My search focused on the actions and skills required to start and scale a business. In addition, I reviewed literature on innovation processes to understand the key traits of successful innovators. Faculty collaboration at various research universities helped guide my search: Harvard University, Massachusetts Institute of Technology, Carnegie Mellon University, University of Michigan, Northwestern University, Stanford University, and the University of Chicago.

Research Phase 2: Defining Selection Criteria

The project included 200 interviews with founders across multiple industries, including technology, retail, energy, health care, media, mobile applications, science, real estate, travel and hospitality, restaurants, and education. (Note: The data set includes business entrepreneurs and a smaller subset of social entrepreneurs and business executives who launched revolutionary initiatives within larger organizations.)

The following criteria helped identify interviewees:

He/she founded an enterprise that has scaled to more than $100 million in revenue and/or served more than 100,000 individuals.

He/she has achieved high-scale growth over a 5-to-10-year period of time.

He/she is currently founder/CEO or still actively involved in management.

He/she came recommended by at least three industry peers.

Research Phase 3: Field Expert Interviews

My research objectives in this phase were threefold: 1) to evaluate the actions and skill sets of highly successful creators; 2) to deepen my understanding of how these individuals approached opportunities in rapidly evolving contexts; and 3) to generate additional individuals to be interviewed that might have been missed in the original target list.

For this phase, I employed a grounded theory method—an approach commonly used in qualitative analysis. Following this methodology, I developed a thorough interview guide with questions used for each interviewee. Targeted data were collected by asking specific but open-ended questions. Interviews took the form of semi-structured interviews asking a set of standard questions but varying follow-up questions depending on the interviewee.

I conducted all interviews personally. Each interview ranged in length from one to three hours. (A small subset were conducted by phone.)

Example questions included:

What is your background, and how did you recognize the opportunity to start your company?

How did you encourage and manage rapid growth of your business?

What updates, adaptations, or obstacles did you overcome to achieve high scale?

What kind of connections with other individuals and/or firms do you have, and how do you cultivate relationships to amplify growth of your enterprise?

Research Phase 4: Pattern Recognition and Analysis

All interviews were recorded and then transcribed. From the interview data collected, key points were marked with a series of codes. Codes of similar content were grouped into concepts. From the concepts, categories were formed to provide the basis for developing a theory of the six essential skills of creators.

In addition, I reviewed hundreds of academic studies and collected more than 5,000 pieces of secondary data including field notes, newspaper and magazine articles, government reports, organization reports, and other materials from site visits. I coded all material using the constant comparative method (line-by-line analysis). I did this manually, as software is not recommended in grounded theory.

Overall, I synthesized nearly 10,000 pages of transcript notes, over 5,000 pages of secondary data, and well over 4,000 pages of academic research including experiments, studies, conceptual arguments, and interviews with academic colleagues. I used the constant comparative method to analyze the data. I developed memos to capture emergent concepts and their relationships. As I conducted additional interviews, I reconceptualized categories and continued to refine the concepts. I used the constant comparative method to reexamine the data against the emerging categories, until the data were saturated and six essential skills had emerged.

Overall, my research points to patterns of action that can be emulated. The ability to start and scale new enterprises can be learned. It is not merely a function of an entrepreneurial mind or elite background or access to specific resources or training. The creators I interviewed repeatedly described behaviors that anyone can practice.

While they differ across industry, these creators share common approaches and skills. Thus, conducting this research and disseminating its findings will place valuable insight in the hands of aspiring creators to strengthen their ability to turn an idea into an enterprise that can achieve massive scale.

REFERENCES

CRACKING THE CODE

Blakely, Sara. Author interview.

Burke, Monte. "Under Armour CEO Kevin Plank and His Underdog Horse Farm." *Forbes*, September 7, 2012. http://www.forbes.com/sites/monteburke/2012/09/07/under-armour-ceo-kevin-plank-and-his-underdog-horse-farm/.

Carr, Austin. "Most Innovative Companies 2012: 19: Airbnb." *Fast Company*, February 7, 2012. http://www.fastcompany.com/3017358/most-innovative-companies-2012/19airbnb.

Chase, Robin. Author interview.

Dessauer, Carin. "Team Player." *Bethesda Magazine*, March–April 2009. http://www.bethesdamagazine.com/Bethesda-Magazine/March-April-2009/Team-Player.

Friedman, Thomas L. "Welcome to the Sharing Economy." *New York Times*, July 20, 2013. http://www.nytimes.com/2013/07/21/opinion/sunday/friedman-welcome-to-the-sharing-economy.html.

"From Rags to Microfiber: The Story of Under Armour." *Sports Illustrated*, April 9, 2009. http://www.si.com/more-sports/2009/04/09/under-armour.

Gebbia, Joe. Author interview.

Heath, Thomas. "Taking on the giants: How Under Armour founder Kevin Plank is going head-to-head with the industry's biggest players." *Washington Post*, January 24, 2010. http://www.washingtonpost.com/wp-dyn/content/article/2010/01/15/AR2010011503033.html.

REFERENCES

Hempel, Jessi. "Airbnb: More than a Place to Crash." *Fortune*, May 3, 2012. http://fortune.com/2012/05/03/airbnb-more-than-a-place-to-crash.

Hoffman, Reid. Author interview.

Holmes, Elizabeth. Author interview.

Langer, Bob. Author interview.

Laskey, Alex. Author interview.

Levchin, Max. Author interview.

Musk, Elon. Author interview.

Omidyar, Pierre. Author interview.

Parloff, Roger. "This CEO's Out for Blood." *Fortune*, June 12, 2014. http://fortune.com/2014/06/12/theranos-blood-holmes.

Plank, Kevin. Author interview.

Plank, Kevin. "How I Did It: Kevin Plank of Under Armour (2003 Column)." *Inc.* Mansueto Ventures, December 1, 2003. http://www.inc.com/magazine/20031201/howididit.html.

Rago, Joseph. "Elizabeth Holmes: The Breakthrough of Instant Diagnosis." *Wall Street Journal*, September 8, 2013. http://online.wsj.com/news/articles/SB10001424127887324123004579055003869574012.

Spector, Mike, Douglas MacMillan, and Evelyn M. Rusli. "TPG-Led Group Closes $450 Million Investment in Airbnb." *WSJ*, April 18, 2014. http://online.wsj.com/news/articles/SB10001424052702304626304579509800267341652.

Stoppelman, Jeremy. Author interview.

Thiel, Peter. Author interview.

Wilhelm, Alex. "If Dropbox's 2013 Revenue Is $200M, an $8B Valuation Is Pretty Steep." *TechCrunch.com*, November 19, 2013. http://techcrunch.com/2013/11/19/if-dropboxs-2013-revenue-is-200m-an-8b-valuation-is-pretty-steep.

FIND THE GAP

Baron, Robert A., and Scott A. Shane. *Entrepreneurship: A Process Perspective.* 2nd ed. Mason, OH: Thomson South-Western, 2007.

Bronson, Po, and Ashley Merryman. "The Creativity Crisis." *Newsweek*, January 23, 2014.

Callaghan, Beth. "Kevin Rose Interviews Elon Musk." *AllThingsD.com*, September 7, 2012. http://allthingsd.com/20120907/kevin-rose-interviews-elon-musk.

Chafkin, Max. "Elon Musk's Guide to the Galaxy." *Inc.*, October 1, 2010. http://www.inc.com/magazine/20101001/elon-musks-guide-to-the-galaxy_pagen_4.html.

Chouinard, Michelle M., Paul L. Harris, and Michael P. Maratsos. "Children's questions: A mechanism for cognitive development." *Monographs of the Society for Research in Child Development* (2007): i-129.

Destro, Jeanne. "Review: Tinkering Spirit Made America Great." Review of *The Tinkerers: The Amateurs, DIYers, and Inventors Who Made America Great*, by

Alec Foege. *Baxter Bulletin (Mountain Home, AR),* February 10, 2013. http://archive.baxterbulletin.com/usatoday/article/1872299.

Dunn, Julie. "Free-Range Burritos: Is This McDonalds?" *New York Times,* September 29, 2002. http://www.nytimes.com/2002/09/29/business/grass-roots-business-free-range-burritos-is-this-mcdonald-s.html.

Ells, Steve. Author interview.

"Elon Musk Profiled: Bloomberg Risk Takers: Video." *Bloomberg,* n.d. http://www.bloomberg.com/video/elon-musk-profiled-bloomberg-risk-takers-_saQce11QCGWrZ9UuCMNBw.html.

Estes, Zachary, and Thomas B. Ward. "The Emergence of Novel Attributes in Concept Modification." *Creativity Research Journal* 14, no. 2 (2002): 149–56.

Frank, Michael C., and Michael Ramscar. "How Do Presentation and Context Influence Representation for Functional Fixedness Tasks?" *Proceedings of the 25th Annual Meeting of the Cognitive Science Society.* Boston: Cognitive Science Society, 2003.

Gentner, Dedre. Author interview.

Getzels, Jacob W. "The Problem of the Problem." In Robin M. Hogarth, ed., *Question Framing and Response Consistency,* 37–49. New Directions for Methodology of Social and Behavioral Science 11. San Francisco: Jossey-Bass, 1982.

Gick, Mary L., and Keith J. Holyoak. "Schema Induction and Analogical Transfer." *Cognitive Psychology* 15, no. 1 (1983): 1–38.

Hennessy, John. Author interview.

Herrin, Jessica. Author interview.

Hoffman, Carl. "Elon Musk, the Rocket Man With a Sweet Ride." Smithsonian.com, December 2012. http://www.smithsonianmag.com/science-nature/elon-musk-the-rocket-man-with-a-sweet-ride-136059680.

Junod, Tom. "Elon Musk SpaceX Interview." *Esquire,* November 15, 2012. http://www.esquire.com/features/americans-2012/elon-musk-interview-1212.

Kamen, Dean. Author interview.

Langer, Robert S. "Langer Lab: Professor Robert Langer." MIT, n.d. http://mit.edu/langerlab/langer.html.

"Launch Manifest." SpaceX. http://www.spacex.com/missions.

Maybank, Alexis. Author interview.

Maybank, Alexis, and Alexandra W. Wilson. *By Invitation Only: How We Built Gilt and Changed the Way Millions Shop.* New York: Portfolio/Penguin, 2012.

Mayfield, Dan. "Battery Industry Analyst Sam Jaffe Skeptical on NM's Chances for Tesla Gigafactory." *Albuquerque Business First,* February 26, 2014. http://www.bizjournals.com/albuquerque/blog/morning-edition/2014/02/analyst-skeptical-nm-tesla-factory.html.

Porter, Jane. "How Stella & Dot Is Giving Old-Fashioned Direct Sales A Mobile Makeover." *Fast Company.* May 2, 2014. http://www.fastcompany.com/3029929/bottom-line/how-stella-dot-is-giving-old-fashioned-direct-sales-a-mobile-makeover.

Rothenberg, Albert. "The Janusian Process in Scientific Creativity." *Creativity Research Journal* 9, no. 2 (1996): 207–31.

Schultz, Howard, and Dori J. Yang. *Pour Your Heart into It: How Starbucks Built a Company One Cup at a Time.* New York: Hyperion, 1997.

Seligson, Hannah. "M.I.T. Lab Hatches Ideas, and Companies, by the Dozens." *New York Times*, November 24, 2012. http://www.nytimes.com/2012/11/25 /business/mit-lab-hatches-ideas-and-companies-by-the-dozens.html.

SpaceX. "Mission Summary: Dragon Becomes First Private Spacecraft to Visit the Space Station." Space Exploration Technologies Corp., June 1, 2012. http:// www.spacex.com/news/2013/02/08/mission-summary.

Stein, Joel. "The Fast-Food Ethicist." *Time*, July 23, 2012. http://content.time.com /time/magazine/article/0,9171,2119329,00.html.

Tice, Carol. "Why Starbucks' VIA Instant Coffee Is Bigger than Frappuccino." *CBSNews.com*, August 9, 2010. http://www.cbsnews.com/news/why-starbucks -via-instant-coffee-is-bigger-than-frappuccino.

Tierney, John. "NASA, We've Got a Problem. But It Can Be Fixed." *New York Times*, April 12, 2010. http://www.nytimes.com/2010/04/13/science/13tier .html.

Vogel, Gretchen. "Working Conditions: A Day in the Life of a Topflight Lab." *Science* 285.5433 (1999): 1531-1532.

Ward, Thomas B. "Cognition, Creativity, and Entrepreneurship." *Journal of Business Venturing* 19, no. 2 (2004): 173–88.

"Welcome to DEKA Research and Development." N.p., http://www.dekaresearch .com/index.shtml.

Wilkis Wilson, Alexandra. Author interview.

DRIVE FOR DAYLIGHT

"Avis Budget Group To Acquire Zipcar For $12.25 Per Share In Cash." Zipcar Inc., January 2, 2013. http://www.zipcar.com/press/releases/avis-budget-group -acquires-zipcar.

Baron Robert. Author interview.

Bartiromo, Maria. "Chobani CEO at Center of Greek Yogurt Craze." *USA Today*, June 16, 2013. http://www.usatoday.com/story/money/columnist/bartiromo /2013/06/16/chobani-ulukaya-yogart/2423611.

Burke, Monte. "Under Armour CEO Kevin Plank and His Underdog Horse Farm." *Forbes*, September 7, 2012. http://www.forbes.com/sites/monteburke /2012/09/07/under-armour-ceo-kevin-plank-and-his-underdog-horse-farm.

Burke, Monte. "Under Armour's About-Face." *Forbes*, February 14, 2011. http:// www.forbes.com/forbes/2011/0214/focus-kevin-plank-under-armour-clothing -about-face.html.

Della Cava, Marco. "Change Agents: Elizabeth Holmes Wants Your Blood." *USA Today*, July 8, 2014. http://www.usatoday.com/story/tech/2014/07/08/change -agents-elizabeth-holmes-theranos-blood-testing-revolution/12183437.

First Round Capital. "How to Win as a First-Time Founder, a Drew Houston Manifesto." *First Round Review*, n.d. http://firstround.com/article/How-to -Win-as-a-First-Time-Founder-a-Drew-Houston-Manifesto.

Friedman, Thomas L. "Welcome to the Sharing Economy." *New York Times*, July 20, 2013. http://www.nytimes.com/2013/07/21/opinion/sunday/friedman -welcome-to-the-sharing-economy.html.

Geron, Tomio. "Airbnb and the Unstoppable Rise of the Share Economy." *Forbes,* January 23, 2013. http://www.forbes.com/sites/tomiogeron/2013/01/23/airbnb -and-the-unstoppable-rise-of-the-share-economy.

Gruley, Bryan. "At Chobani, the Turkish King of Greek Yogurt." *Bloomberg Businessweek,* January 31, 2013. http://www.businessweek.com/articles /2013-01-31/at-chobani-the-turkish-king-of-greek-yogurt.

Heath, Thomas. "Taking on the Giants: How Under Armour Founder Kevin Plank Is Going Head-to-Head with the Industry's Biggest Players." *Washington Post*, January 24, 2010. http://www.washingtonpost.com/wp-dyn /content/article/2010/01/15/AR2010011503033.html.

Hippel, Eric von. Author interview.

Hippel, Eric von, Susumu Ogawa, and Jeroen P. J. de Jong. "The Age of the Consumer-Innovator." *MIT Sloan Management Review*, Fall 2011. http:// sloanreview.mit.edu/article/the-age-of-the-consumer-innovator.

Hippel, Eric von, Stefan Thomke, and Mary Sonnack. "Creating Breakthroughs at 3M." *Harvard Business Review* 77, no. 5 (September-October 1999).

Hong, Kaylene. "Dropbox Reaches 300M Users." *The Next Web*, May 29, 2014. http://thenextweb.com/insider/2014/05/29/dropbox-reaches-300m-users -adding-100m-users-just-six-months.

Houston, Drew. Author interview.

Isaacson, Walter. "The Real Leadership Lessons of Steve Jobs." *Harvard Business Review*, April 2012. http://hbr.org/2012/04/the-real-leadership-lessons-of -steve-jobs.

Isaacson, Walter. *Steve Jobs*. New York: Simon & Schuster, 2011.

Koo, Minjung, and Ayelet Fishbach. "Dynamics of Self-Regulation: How (Un) Accomplished Goal Actions Affect Motivation." *Journal of Personality and Social Psychology* 94, no. 2 (2008): 183–95.

Levy, Justin R. *Facebook Marketing: Designing Your Next Marketing Campaign.* Indianapolis, Ind: Que, 2010.

Louie, Gilman. Author interview.

McGirt, Ellen. "Facebook's Mark Zuckerberg: Hacker. Dropout. CEO." *Fast Company*, May 1, 2007. http://www.fastcompany.com/59441/facebooks-mark -zuckerberg-hacker-dropout-ceo?utm_source=facebook.

Murray, David K. *Plan B: How to Hatch a Second Plan That's Always Better than Your First*. New York: Free Press, 2011.

Plank, Kevin. "How I Did It: Kevin Plank of Under Armour." *Inc.*, December 1, 2003. http://www.inc.com/magazine/20031201/howididit.html.

Rahman, Hosain. Author interview.

REFERENCES

Roper, Caitlin. "This Woman Invented a Way to Run 30 Lab Tests on Only One Drop of Blood." *Wired*, February 18, 2014. http://www.wired.com/2014/02/elizabeth-holmes-theranos.

Sacks, Danielle. "The Sharing Economy." *Fast Company*, April 18, 2011. http://www.fastcompany.com/1747551/sharing-economy.

Sánchez, José C., Tania Carballo, and Andrea Gutiérrez. "The Entrepreneur from a Cognitive Approach." *Psicothema* 23, no. 3 (2011): 433–38.

Steiner, Christopher. "The $700 Million Yogurt Startup." *Forbes*, September 8, 2011. http://www.forbes.com/sites/christophersteiner/2011/09/08/the-700-million-yogurt-startup/2.

FLY THE OODA LOOP

Baer, Drake. "How LinkedIn's Reid Hoffman Jumped off a Cliff and Built an Airplane." *Fast Company*, May 17, 2013. http://www.fastcompany.com/3009831/bottom-line/how-linkedins-reid-hoffman-jumped-off-a-cliff-and-built-an-airplane.

Boyd, J.R. 1976–1996. Unpublished briefings under the name "A Discourse on winning and losing": "Introduction" (1996), "Patterns of conflict" (1986), "Organic design for command and control" (1987), "Strategic game of ? and ?" (1987), "Destruction and creation" (1976), and "The essence of winning and Losing" (1996) available via Defence and the National Interest http://www.d-n-i.net/second_level/boyd_military.htm.

Cloud, John. "The YouTube Gurus." *Time*, December 25, 2006. http://content.time.com/time/printout/0,8816,1570795,00.html#.

Coram, Robert. *Boyd: The Fighter Pilot Who Changed the Art of War*. Boston: Little, Brown, 2002.

Greenberg, Andy. "How a 'Deviant' Philosopher Built Palantir, a CIA-Funded Data-Mining Juggernaut." *Forbes*, August 14, 2013. http://www.forbes.com/sites/andygreenberg/2013/08/14/agent-of-intelligence-how-a-deviant-philosopher-built-palantir-a-cia-funded-data-mining-juggernaut.

Hammond, Grant T. *The Mind of War: John Boyd and American Security*. Washington, DC: Smithsonian Institution Press, 2001.

Hammonds, Keith H. "The Strategy of the Fighter Pilot." *Fast Company*, May 31, 2002. http://www.fastcompany.com/44983/strategy-fighter-pilot.

Hardy, Quentin. "Unlocking Secrets, if Not Its Own Value." *New York Times*, May 31, 2014. http://www.nytimes.com/2014/06/01/business/unlocking-secrets-if-not-its-own-value.html.

Helft, Miguel. "It Pays to Have Pals in Silicon Valley." *New York Times*, October 17, 2006. http://www.nytimes.com/2006/10/17/technology/17paypal.html.

House Armed Services Committee. "United States Military Reform after Operation Desert Storm." Hearing, April 30, 1991. U.S. House of Representatives. http://pogoblog.typepad.com/files/reform-perspective-on-the-gulf-war-hasc-1991-hearing.pdf.

Jackson, Eric M. *The PayPal Wars: Battles with eBay, the Media, the Mafia, and the Rest of Planet Earth*. Medford, OR: WND Books, 2012.

Koetsier, John. "From $1.5B to Half a Trillion Dollars: PayPal Celebrates a 10th Anniversary." *Reuters*, July 8, 2012. http://www.reuters.com/article/2012/07/08/idUS181564047920120708.

Lilien, Gary L., et al. "Performance Assessment of the Lead User Idea-Generation Process for New Product Development." *Management Science* 48, no. 8 (2002): 1042–59.

Livingston, Jessica. *Founders at Work: Stories of Startups' Early Days*. Berkeley, CA: Apress, 2008.

Lonsdale, Joe. Author interview.

Mac, Ryan. "CIA-Funded Data-Miner Palantir Not Yet Profitable but Looking for $8 Billion Valuation." *Forbes*, August 16, 2013. http://www.forbes.com/sites/ryanmac/2013/08/16/cia-funded-data-miner-palantir-not-yet-profitable-but-looking-for-8-billion-valuation.

MacMillan, Douglas. "PayPal Co-Founder Max Levchin Raises $45 Million for Startup Affirm." *Digits* blog, *Wall Street Journal*, June 9, 2014. http://blogs.wsj.com/digits/2014/06/09/paypal-co-founder-max-levchin-raises-45-million-for-startup-affirm.

O'Brien, Jeffrey M. "Meet the PayPal Mafia." *CNN Money*, November 26, 2007. http://cnnfn.cnn.com/2007/11/13/magazines/fortune/paypal_mafia.fortune/index.htm.

Packer, George. "Peter Thiel's Rise to Wealth and Libertarian Futurism." *New Yorker*, November 28, 2011. http://www.newyorker.com/reporting/2011/11/28/111128fa_fact_packer?currentPage=all.

Parr, Ben. "Easter Egg: Yelp Is the iPhone's First Augmented Reality App." Mashable.com, August 27, 2009. http://mashable.com/2009/08/27/yelp-augmented-reality.

Richmond, Riva. "Yelp Co-Founder Jeremy Stoppelman on Innovating and Staying Relevant." *Entrepreneur*, September 10, 2012. http://www.entrepreneur.com/blog/224338#.

Rininger, Tyson V. *F-15 Eagle at War*. Minneapolis, MN: Zenith Press, 2009.

Roush, Wade. "Yammer Is Not Just Facebook for Enterprises: A Deep Dive with CEO David Sacks." *Xconomy*, October 13, 2011. http://www.xconomy.com/san-francisco/2011/10/13/yammer-is-not-just-facebook-for-enterprises-a-deep-dive-with-ceo-david-sacks/2.

Rowan, David. "Reid Hoffman: The network philosopher." *Wired UK*, March 1, 2012. http://www.wired.co.uk/magazine/archive/2012/04/features/reid-hoffman-network-philosopher.

Rusli, Evelyn M. "Reid Hoffman of LinkedIn Has Become the Go-To Guy of Tech." *New York Times*, November 5, 2011. http://www.nytimes.com/2011/11/06/business/reid-hoffman-of-linkedin-has-become-the-go-to-guy-of-tech.html.

Sacks, David. Author interview.

REFERENCES

Sacks, David. "The Answers to All Your Questions (in Under 20 Minutes)" (video). *Khosla Ventures*, May 20, 2013. http://www.khoslaventures.com/new -sales-models-david-sacks.

Swisher, Kara. "PayPal Co-Founder Levchin Launches New Payments Startup, Affirm." AllThingsD.com, February 26, 2013. http://allthingsd.com/20130226 /exclusive-paypal-co-founder-levchin-launches-new-payments-startup-affirm.

Tweney, Dylan. "How PayPal Gave Rise to a Silicon Valley Mafia." *Wired*, November 15, 2007. http://www.wired.com/2007/11/how-paypal-gave.

FAIL WISELY

Asseily, Alex. Author interview.

Carolan, Shawn. Author interview.

Chafkin, Max. "Elon Musk's Guide to the Galaxy." *Inc.*, October 1, 2010. http:// www.inc.com/magazine/20101001/elon-musks-guide-to-the-galaxy_pagen_4 .html.

Chung, Patrick. Author interview.

Cohler, Matt. Author interview.

Cuddy, Amy J. C., Kyle T. Doherty, and Maarten W. Bos. "OPOWER: Increasing Energy Efficiency Through Normative Influence (A)." *Harvard Business School* Case 911-016, September 2010. (Revised January 2012.)

Davis, Joshua. "How Elon Musk Turned Tesla into the Car Company of the Future." *Wired*, September 27, 2010. http://www.wired.com/2010/09/ff_tesla /all/1.

Dow, Steven P., Kate Heddleston, and Scott R. Klemmer. "The Efficacy of Prototyping Under Time Constraints." *Proceedings of the Seventh ACM Conference on Creativity and Cognition.* New York: Association for Computing Machinery, 2009.

Dweck, Carol S. Author interview.

Dweck, Carol S. "Caution—Praise Can Be Dangerous." *American Educator* 23, no. 1 (1999): 4–9.

Dyer, Jeff, Hal B. Gregersen, and Clayton M. Christensen. *The Innovator's DNA: Mastering the Five Skills of Disruptive Innovators.* Boston: Harvard Business School Press, 2011.

Gray, Dave. "Experimentation Is the New Planning." *Fast Company*, September 14, 2012. http://www.fastcompany.com/3001275/experimentation-new -planning.

Hastings, Reed. "An Explanation and Some Reflections." Netflix US & Canada Blog, Netflix. September 18, 2011. blog.netflix.com/2011/09/explanation-and -some-reflections.html.

Hudson, Charles. Author interview.

Kasperkevic, Jana. "Elon Musk and Richard Branson's Best Advice for Entrepreneurs." *Inc.*, August 8, 2013. http://www.inc.com/jana-kasperkevic /google-hangout-advice-elon-musk-richard-branson.html.

Kelley, David. Author interview.

Laskey, Alex. "How Behavioral Science Can Lower Your Energy Bill" (video). TED Talk, February 2013. https://www.ted.com/talks/alex_laskey_how _behavioral_science_can_lower_your_energy_bill.

Lawler, Richard. "Netflix Tops 40 Million Customers Total, More Paid US Subscribers than HBO." *Engadget*, October 21, 2013. http://www.engadget .com/2013/10/21/netflix-q3-40-million-total.

MacKenzie, Angus. "2013 Motor Trend Car of the Year: Tesla Model S." *Motor Trend*, January 2013. http://www.motortrend.com/oftheyear/car/1301_2013 _motor_trend_car_of_the_year_tesla_model_s.

Neeleman, David. Author interview.

Newsom, Gavin. Author interview.

Nolan, Jessica M., P. W. Schultz, Robert B. Cialdini, Noah J. Goldstein, and Vladas Griskevicius. "Normative Social Influence Is Underdetected." *Personality and Social Psychology Bulletin* 34, no. 7 (2008): 913–23.

Peters, Sara. "Dell World: Elon Musk's Innovation Tips." *Enterprise Efficiency*, December 12, 2013. http://www.enterpriseefficiency.com/author.asp?section _id=1134&doc_id=270408.

Schlangenstein, Mary. "JetBlue CEO Could Leave Airline When Contract Expires Next Year." *Dallas Morning News*, May 7, 2014. http://www.dallasnews.com /business/airline-industry/20140507-jetblue-ceo-could-leave-airline-when -contract-expires-next-year.ece.

Schmit, Julie. "Do You Use More Energy than Your Neighbors?" *USA Today*, January 2, 2010. http://usatoday30.usatoday.com/money/industries/energy /2010-02-01-homeenergy01_st_n.htm.

Schultz, P. Wesley, et al. "The Constructive, Destructive, and Reconstructive Power of Social Norms." *Psychological Science* 18, no. 5 (2007): 429–34.

Skillman, Peter. "Peter Skillman at Gel 2007" (video). April 19, 2007. http://vimeo .com/39910683.

Stewart, James B. "Netflix Looks Back on Its Near-Death Spiral." *New York Times*, April 26, 2013. http://www.nytimes.com/2013/04/27/business/netflix-looks -back-on-its-near-death-spiral.html.

Tinjum, Aaron. "We've now saved 5 terawatt-hours. That's enough energy to power New Hampshire for a year." *Opower*, July 22, 2014. http://blog.opower .com/tag/terawatt-hour/.

Yates, Dan. Author interview.

Zuckerman, Laurence. "Ambitious Low-Fare Carrier Names Itself JetBlue Airways." *New York Times*, July 15, 1999. http://www.nytimes.com/1999/07/15 /business/ambitious-low-fare-carrier-names-itself-jetblue-airways.html.

NETWORK MINDS

"Best Lifestyle Trackers: Jawbone UP." MSN, August 19, 2013. http://technology.ie .msn.com/best-lifestyle-trackers-1?page=2.

REFERENCES

Bingham, Alph. Author interview.

Black, Jane. "At Some Schools, Tastier Trays Come at a Price." *Washington Post,* September 30, 2009. http://www.washingtonpost.com/wp-dyn/content/article /2009/09/29/AR2009092900741.html.

Boesler, Matthew. "Tom Ryan, CEO of Threadless: Social Web Commerce and the Atrium Platform." *Benzinga,* July 29, 2011. http://www.benzinga.com/general /movers-shakers/11/07/1818198/tom-ryan-ceo-of-threadless-social-web -commerce-and-the-atrium-p.

Bogard, Travis. "Jawbone Now Works with Nest." The Jawbone Blog, Jawbone, June 23, 2014. https://jawbone.com/blog/jawbone-up-works-with-nest.

Dietz, Doug. Author interview.

Dietz, Doug. "Transforming Healthcare for Children and Their Families" (video). TEDx Talk, San Jose, CA, 2012. http://tedxtalks.ted.com/video/TEDxSanJose CA-2012-Doug-Dietz-T.

Dodgson, Mark. "Learning from Britain's Secret Decryption Centre, Bletchley Park." Australian Broadcasting Corporation, December 6, 2013. http://www .abc.net.au/radionational/programs/ockhamsrazor/learning-from-britains -secret-decryption-centre-bletchley-park/5136522.

"Gartner Predicts Over 70 Percent of Global 2000 Organisations Will Have at Least One Gamified Application by 2014." Gartner Inc., N.p., November 9, 2011. http://www.gartner.com/newsroom/id/1844115.

Groos Richmond, Kristin. Author interview.

Guimerà, Roger, Brian Uzzi, Jarrett Spiro, and Luís A. Amaral. "Team Assembly Mechanisms Determine Collaboration Network Structure and Team Performance." *Science* 308, no. 5722 (2005): 697–702.

Holden, Mark. Author interview.

Horowitz, Sara. Author interview.

"InnoCentive Solvers Make a Difference in Rural Africa and India." InnoCentive, March 3, 2008. http://www.innocentive.com/innocentive-solvers-make -difference-rural-africa-and-india.

"Innovation Management | Crowdsourcing | Challenges | Competitions." N.p., n.d. http://www.innocentive.com/.

"Jawbone Acquires Visere and Massive Health." *mHealth Spot,* February 4, 2013. http://mhealthspot.com/2013/02/jawbone-acquires-visere-massive-health.

Jeppesen, Lars Bo, and Karim R. Lakhani. "Marginality and Problem-Solving Effectiveness in Broadcast Search." *Organization Science* 21, no. 5 (2010): 1016–33.

Kanellos, Michael. "Silicon Valley Entrepreneurs Aim to Disrupt Food Industry." *Forbes,* January 23, 2012. http://www.forbes.com/sites/michaelkanellos/2012 /01/23/why-are-entrepreneurs-flocking-to-food.

Kelley, David, and Tom Kelley. *Creative Confidence: Unleashing the Creative Potential within Us All.* New York: Crown Business, 2013.

Kembel, George. Author interview.

Kothari, Akshay. Author interview.

Lakhani, Karim R. Author interview.

Loyd, Denise Lewin, et al. "Social Category Diversity Promotes Premeeting Elaboration: The Role of Relationship Focus." *Organization Science* 24, no. 3 (2013): 757–72.

Maxmen, Amy. "Driving Innovation: Ready, Set, Go!" *Cell* 140, no. 2 (2010): 171–73.

McGonigal, Jane. "Making Alternate Reality the New Business Reality." *Harvard Business Review* 86, no. 2 (2008): 29.

———. *Reality Is Broken: Why Games Make Us Better and How They Can Change the World.* New York: Penguin, 2011.

Nickell, Jake. Author interview.

"Nobel Prizes and Laureates." *Nobelprize.org.* Nobel Media AB, http://www .nobelprize.org/nobel_prizes/.

Page, Scott E. *The Difference: How the Power of Diversity Creates Better Groups, Firms, Schools, and Societies.* Princeton, NJ: Princeton University Press, 2007.

Pang, Alex Soojung-Kim. "Mighty Mouse." *Stanford Magazine*, Stanford University, April 2002. https://alumni.stanford.edu/get/page/magazine /article/?article_id=37694.

Papapostolou, David, Matt Norton, and Sean Garbett. "2014 Contingent Market Forecasts." Staffing Industry Analysts webinar, November 13, 2013. http:// www.staffingindustry.com/content/download/155422/6074769/file/Forecast %20webinar%20131113%20FINAL.pdf.

Phillips, Katherine W. Author interview.

Phillips, Katherine W., Katie A. Liljenquist, and Margaret A. Neale. "Is the Pain Worth the Gain? The Advantages and Liabilities of Agreeing with Socially Distinct Newcomers." *Personality and Social Psychology Bulletin* 35, no. 3 (2009): 336–50.

Rasmussen, Eric. Author interview.

Saenz Tobey, Kirsten. Author interview.

Sawchuk, Hillary, and Kelly Kane. "Threadless Founder Jake Nickell." *A Drink With,* April 4, 2013. http://adrinkwith.com/jake-nickell.

Stern, Joanna. "Jawbone UP Fitness Gadget Back on Sale with Fixed Up Hardware and a New App." ABC News, November 13, 2012. http://abcnews.go.com /Technology/jawbone-fitness-gadget-back-sale-fixed-hardware-app/story?id =17704171.

Tischler, Linda. "Ideo's David Kelley on 'Design Thinking.'" *Fast Company,* February 1, 2009. http://www.fastcompany.com/1139331/ideos-david-kelley -design-thinking.

Truong, Alice. "Holiday Gifts: Techie Picks for the Health Nut." *USA Today,* November 26, 2012. http://www.usatoday.com/story/tech/columnist/2012/11 /24/holiday-gifts-techie-picks-for-health-fitness/1713025.

REFERENCES

U.S. Government Accountability Office. *Employment Arrangements: Improved Outreach Could Help Ensure Proper Worker Classification.* Washington, DC: U.S. Government Accountability Office, 2006. http://www.gao.gov/products /GAO-06-656.

University of Washington. "Computer Game's High Score Could Earn the Nobel Prize in Medicine." *Science Daily,* May 9, 2008. http://www.sciencedaily.com /releases/2008/05/080508122520.htm.

Uzzi, Brian. Author interview.

Zoran Popović. Author interview.

GIFT SMALL GOODS

Aoki, Naomi. "The Crusader MIT Scientist Robert Langer Doesn't Believe in Science for Science's Sake. He Sees It as a Means to Change the World—and He Has." *Boston Globe,* May 25, 2003.

Arnaud, Celia H. "Big-Picture Thinker." *Chemical and Engineering News* 90, no. 13 (March 26, 2012). http://cen.acs.org/articles/90/i13/Big-Picture-Thinker .html.

Blanding, Michael. "The Bioconductor." *One* 4, no. 1 (Fall-Winter 2011). Carey Business School, Johns Hopkins University. http://carey.jhu.edu/one/2011/fall /the-bioconductor.

Chivers, Tom. "Martin Nowak: A Helping Hand for Evolution." *Telegraph,* March 15, 2011. http://www.telegraph.co.uk/science/evolution/8382449/Martin -Nowak-a-helping-hand-for-evolution.html.

Christakis, Nicholas A., and James H. Fowler. "Social Contagion Theory: Examining Dynamic Social Networks and Human Behavior." *Statistics in Medicine* 32, no. 4 (2013): 556–77.

Flynn, Francis J. "How Much Should I Give and How Often? The Effects of Generosity and Frequency of Favor Exchange on Social Status and Productivity." *Academy of Management Journal* 46, no. 5 (2003): 539–53.

Fowler, James H. Author interview.

Fowler, James H., and Nicholas A. Christakis. "Cooperative Behavior Cascades in Human Social Networks." *Proceedings of the National Academy of Sciences* 107, no. 12 (2010): 5334–8.

Harman, Oren. "How Evolution Explains Altruism." *New York Times,* Sunday Book Review, April 8, 2011. http://www.nytimes.com/2011/04/10/books /review/book-review-supercooperators-by-martin-a-nowak.html.

Hoffman, Reid. "Big Think Interview with Reid Hoffman." *Big Think,* November 4, 2009. http://bigthink.com/videos/big-think-interview-with-reid-hoffman.

"Kiva Announces $1 Million in Free Trials Funded by Reid Hoffman, Founder of LinkedIn | Kiva." *Kiva,* March 13, 2012. http://www.kiva.org/press/releases /release_20130114-3.

Kunz, Phillip R., and Michael Woolcott. "Season's Greetings: From My Status to Yours." *Social Science Research* 5, no. 3 (1976): 269–78.

"Langer Lab: Professor Robert Langer." Massachusetts Institute of Technology. Last updated June 20, 2014. http://web.mit.edu/langerlab/langer.html.

Levy, Ellen. Author interview.

Nonacs, Peter. "Reciprocity, Reputation and Nepotism." *American Scientist* 99 (2011): 422–24.

Nowak, Martin A. Author interview.

Nowak, Martin A. "Why We Help: The Evolution of Cooperation." *Scientific American* 307, no. 1 (July 2012).

Nowak, Martin A., and Roger Highfield. *Supercooperators: Altruism, Evolution, and Why We Need Each Other to Succeed.* New York: Free Press, 2011.

Pearson, Helen. "Profile: Being Bob Langer." *Nature*, March 4, 2009. http://www .nature.com/news/2009/090304/full/458022a.html.

Rand, David G. Author interview.

Rand, David G., Samuel Arbesman, and Nicholas A. Christakis. "Dynamic Social Networks Promote Cooperation in Experiments with Humans." *Proceedings of the National Academy of Sciences* 108, no. 48 (2011): 19193–8.

Radowitz, John V. "Bionic vocal cord may restore the sound of Dame Julie." *The Independent.* N.p., August 21, 2012. http://www.independent.co.uk/news /science/bionic-vocal-cord-may-restore-the-sound-of-dame-julie-8063484 .html.

"Reid Hoffman." *Who Owns Facebook? The Definitive Who's Who Guide to Facebook Wealth*, n.d. http://whoownsfacebook.com.

Reuell, Peter. "Nice Guys Can Finish First." *Harvard Gazette*, November 14, 2011. http://news.harvard.edu/gazette/story/2011/11/social-networks.

"Robert Langer Biography." American Academy of Achievement. Last updated December 19, 2013. http://www.achievement.org/autodoc/page/lan1bio-1.

Rowan, David. "Reid Hoffman: The Network Philosopher." *Wired UK*, March 1, 2012. http://www.wired.co.uk/magazine/archive/2012/04/features/reid -hoffman-network-philosopher.

Rusli, Evelyn M. "A King of Connections Is Tech's Go-To Guy." *New York Times*, November 5, 2011. http://www.nytimes.com/2011/11/06/business/reid -hoffman-of-linkedin-has-become-the-go-to-guy-of-tech.html.

Seligson, Hannah. "M.I.T. Lab Hatches Ideas, and Companies, by the Dozens." *New York Times*, November 24, 2012. http://www.nytimes.com/2012/11/25 /business/mit-lab-hatches-ideas-and-companies-by-the-dozens.html.

"SPANX - Leg Up Official Rules." *Spanx.* http://pages.email.spanx.com/legup/.

Tsvetkova, Milena. "The Science of 'Paying It Forward'." *New York Times*, N.p., March 2014. http://www.nytimes.com/2014/03/16/opinion/sunday/the-science -of-paying-it-forward.html?_r=0.

Vogel, Gretchen. "A Day in the Life of a Topflight Lab." *Science* 285, no. 5433 (1999): 1531–2.

Weedman, Jeff. Author interview.

CONCLUSION

Antonucci, Mike. "The Whole World in His Plans." *Stanford Magazine*, Stanford University, April 2012. https://alumni.stanford.edu/get/page/magazine/article/?article_id=47654.

"Jeff Skoll." *Participant Media*, n.d. http://www.participantmedia.com/company/jeff-skoll.

Omidyar, Pierre. "How Pierre Omidyar Turned an Idealistic Notion into Billions of Dollars." As told to Issie Lapowsky. *Inc.*, December 2013–January 2014. http://www.inc.com/magazine/201312/pierre-omidyar/ebay-inspiration-more-effective-than-delegation.html.

Plank, Kevin. Author interview.

Shulgan, Chris. "Mr. Skoll Goes to Hollywood." *Globe and Mail*, February 21, 2006, last updated December 30, 2010. http://www.theglobeandmail.com/report-on-business/mr-skoll-goes-to-hollywood/article1321720.

Skoll, Jeff. Author interview.

Skoll, Jeff. "My Journey into Movies That Matter." TED Talk, March 2007. https://www.ted.com/talks/jeff_skoll_makes_movies_that_make_change.

INDEX

Page references in italics indicate illustrations.

ABOUT THE AUTHOR

Amy Wilkinson is a strategic advisor, entrepreneur, and lecturer at the Stanford Graduate School of Business. She frequently addresses corporate, association, and university audiences on entrepreneurial leadership. She also advises startups and large corporations on innovation and business strategy. Her career spans leadership roles with McKinsey & Company and JP Morgan and as founder of a small foreign-based export company. Wilkinson has served as a White House Fellow in the Office of the United States Trade Representative and as a senior fellow at the Harvard Kennedy School. Readers can learn more about her work at www.amywilkinson.com.